The Awakening Letters
Volume Two

The Awakening Letters Volume Two

by
Cynthia Sandys

Selected and edited
by
Rosamond Lehmann

Saffron Walden
The C. W. Daniel Company Limited

First published in 1986 by
The C. W. Daniel Company Limited
1 Church Path, Saffron Walden, Essex, England

© Cynthia Sandys and Rosamond Lehmann 1986

ISBN 0 850207 177 9

Cover:
Left hand picture – Sally, daughter of
Rosamond Lehmann
Right hand picture – Patricia, daughter of
Cynthia Sandys

Designed by Jim Reader
Production in association with
Book Production Consultants, Cambridge
Typeset by Ann Buchan (Typesetters), Surrey

Printed and bound in Great Britain by Clays Ltd, St Ives PLC

Foreword

Here at last is the long awaited Volume Two of the Awakening Letters. Readers familiar with the two booklets, 'Letters from our Daughters' published by the College of Psychic Studies will already have been introduced to Cynthia's daughter, Patricia, and my own daughter, Sally, and will understand why we agree that their photographs should appear on the jacket of this book. They mark the beginning in 1958, of Cynthia's and my own long friendship, and our first joint appearance in print. More of their letters appear in the present volume, as the did in Volume One; but Cynthia's area of communication continues to spread and widen, including other relatives and friends. . . . Some distinguished during their earth lives, some not at all.

The climate has so altered during the last 25 years, that, the occasionally 'way out' material that Cynthia receives and records is now accepted in a way almost impossible to imagine when we first met: when she helped radically to change and illuminate my spiritual outlook.

In one of his letters to me, that great seer W. Tudor Pole said of her, 'she is the purest mental channel known to me'.

Her method, is, of course, the same: she sits quietly, her writing pad on her lap; and, after a period of deep meditation, she starts rapidly to write. She gives the impression of intense stillness and concentration, and the words come in an uninterrupted flow, pouring into her mind, so she says, through the chakra between the eyes (the third eye) and through the crown centre.

As each page is covered with her delicate unpunctuated script, I take it from her . . . when I am present, and wait until the power runs out, and she lays down her pen. Afterwards we read the whole letter through together, copy it and punctuate it. But nowadays I am only one of many whose debt to her for enlightenment and consolation is immeasurable.

It has not been possible to arrange these letters in any definite order, apart from the Suicide sequence and the letters Barbara Lea and Edith Wood. It seems to me that this is not a book to read straight through from the first page to the last: but to be assimilated in small spiritual and psychic doses; so to speak; otherwise the effect of the information given might be too overwhelming.

Rosamond Lehmann

Preface

'When Earth breaks up, and Heaven expands
How will the change strike me and you,
In the House not made with hands?'

'Aye, there's the rub'

Here are a few further *Awakening Letters* covering some descriptions of our probable future lives and faculties. My daughter Patricia (or Pat) often makes the link for me, and of course Sally, Rosamond Lehmann's daughter. We use the same method of meditation, and when I feel that I have extended my aura (as they put it) to receive the link with their thinking matter I write and write until the power ceases.

Joe   my brother, Sir Alvary Gascoigne.
Patricia   my daughter, Mrs Pepys Cockerell.
Sally   Rosamond Lehmann's daughter.
My Mother   Mrs Gascoigne.
Arthur   My husband, Lt. Colonel R.E. Baron Sandys.
Canon Shepherd   Translator of several books by Rudolf Steiner.
Barbara Lea   An old friend of mine.
Olga   Lady Byatt also a very old friend.
Zed Adamski   my brother-in-law. Author of *Flying Saucers have landed*.
W. T. P.   Wellesley Tudor Pole

Cynthia Sandys

JOAN OF ARC: ORLEANS

3rd May 1967   *From my mother*
I feel I must write from here and tell you about Joan; you must not leave this country without knowing and feeling the tremendous impact she had on France and England.

Joan was, of course, as Initiate, a Christed One. She came and succeeded in the task, and then like Christ she died to complete the sacrifice. It was a gift of complete resignation. You can compare the two lives in spite of the very scanty knowledge you possess.

The moral fibre of France was so low at this time, that they were frightened of her strength and gave her up to a foreign power just as the Jews gave Jesus to the Romans. Joan submitted to the whole horror of sacrifice; she completes the circle of male and female initiation on the earth plane. It is most astonishing that her amazing power has never been truly recognized. She had no need to kill in battle, she appeared . . . the Maid was among them, and the enemy dispersed. She never took life in any form. Let your thoughts as a woman reach out to the supreme life of giving.

Joan is very strongly in the atmosphere here in Orleans. I have seen her once in the high etheric, and once on the lower etheric over this city. She links in mind with all who appeal to her. I was not incarnating at the time when she lived here, but Douglas was, and I am going to hand over to him.

Yes I do remember scenes which your presence here, combined with Granny have helped me to recover. I was with the French army and of course we all laughed about this fanatical girl. We thought she was mad, but she had a whimsical attraction about her that one couldn't throw off. She found the King all on her own, and made him pluck up courage to use her among his rabble of an army. I know we all felt she gave us courage. I can see one extraordinary scene when her presence seemed to make the enemy vanish. We were all a bit afraid of her, she was uncanny. I wish I'd known more or been in touch since; but now Granny has opened my eyes to her real power I am going to make a contact.

4th May 1967

We must say another word about Joan, she is so near to this city now, at the time of her fête of recognition when thoughts are turned towards her almost legendary past. Now begins the era when her power is going to be re-discovered. It has lain for so long in the ether due mainly to the fault of the Church who would not recognize her and did all they could to submerge her influence. Now the etheric contact with earth is growing stronger, and the Church is losing power because it will not change and co-operate, and so it is being superceded by an inflow of instinctive intention. Joan is among the leaders of this superb fountain of power.

I was near to her when she received the etheric conditions of this city, and we all laughed at the incongruities everywhere. Joan is full of laughter. She is the happiest person imaginable; she knows its value on all planes. Laughter sets up a series of bubbles in the ether which reflect light and colour like a waterfall to drop in tinkling cascades of thought into the ether. We visited the churches with her and she blessed them with her ray of love. Then, turning to us who were all trying to impress the ray more firmly on the ether she said: 'They were always against me here, and the "vibes" are hard to change.' But as she spoke I saw a film of light gathering over the altar, and I asked what particular form of vibe she was creating? They answered me, 'Enlightenment and Freedom'. Man must be freed from these dogmatic bonds and allow the God-Power to move as it will among the people.

Ma, that was Florence Nightingale.

Patricia
When someone dies in hospital with one of these diseases (T.B., cancer, etc.) two different teams go to work. One to help the spirit body, and the other to guard and remove the etheric body without any bruise or injury. This may sound odd but if the etheric body is bruised or torn, the vital current escapes – in other words, a short circuit – and the whole thing shuts up, and in the flick of an eyelash it's gone. So this is very, very skilled work, and intensely fascinating. You know how much I loved watching and dissecting when I was a Nature Cure student in Edinburgh, so this is absolutely meat and drink to me. I spend hours and hours in Flo's laboratory.

Sometimes when the etheric has been detached quite perfectly we are able to keep it alive for a long time artificially. It's like a person in hospital, yet in reality it's only the reflection of a person and a disease. We can watch the growth of the disease which goes on quite normally, while the reflection of the personality remains strong. We can talk and laugh with this shadow person who is, of course, really operating from the spirit body elsewhere, while this other body is acting like a loud speaker; which is, in a sense, what we all are, our greater selves are so much greater than the strange distortions which come through on the physical plane. But, on the physical, all bodies are in close union, while on the etheric, they have each become detached, and it is only a sort of automatic response.

My Mother, a few days later, who had known 'Flo' as an austere elder cousin.
27th January 1958
I should like to go back to the subject of healing and Flo Nightingale. I found Flo very much the same as when I first remembered her, a very assured person, spare of figure, active and almost hostile to any weakness, and with a habit of going like a spear thrust to the root of the matter. I was always a little frightened of her, she was so austere. Now that has all gone and we laughed a lot when I told her how shy she had always made me feel. I can't tell you how she works, like a steam engine all the time. My Father calls her the Non-stop Flo!

3

Flo teaches us how to look after etheric bodies, and this would answer the needs of the etheric body when attached to the physical, a thing which is very seldom considered. It needs music, light and colour primarily, and when fit, it re-sets itself in alignment with the physical. Exercise, or any active movement stimulates it and raises the vibrations. The etheric loves movement, so motoring and flying can give it the air flow which acts like a tonic. It's very interesting to watch the etheric when it has been separated from the physical.

Flo does much of her diagnosis during the sleep of the patient. She has the most wonderful magnetic fingers. She never touches the etheric body, but she can draw out certain portions and examine them, and can recognize the organs even in their shadowy, embryonic state. She has the most extraordinary flair for sensing the trouble. I often watch her for hours as I stand with the power group. Flo breathes up our vital energy and focuses it upon the disease. This method is often most successful and a great deal of healing is done this way.

But in the cases where healing is not possible; she visits the patient and notes the exact condition of the etheric, as it lies during sleep or unconsciousness about a foot above the physical body. When death occurs during this condition, it is very much easier to separate the bodies. One only has to break the silver cord, in the same way as a nurse breaks the cord when a child is born into physical life. But the etheric body has to be treated with great care, no shock vibration of any kind must reach it. The etheric is generally left in a horizontal position, reminding Patricia of a hospital case, as each one is surrounded by a cushion of light, giving the effect of a couch or bed.

4

SATURN

7 March 1961   *Patricia*
When the crisis was over I left. I went right away. I don't suggest that God is not everywhere, but the niggling littleness of humanity drives God-ful-ness into the finer recesses of the ether where we find them, and you have to reach for them through prayer.

Isn't it odd that laughter and fun should be cut out of religion? Laughter is the very essence of God-power, it releases us, it breaks the tension and puts tears in their proper place.

I went along, because I wanted to be free in the biggest sense I could attain, but as the fascination of all around me awoke thoughts which leapt out from my aura instead of turning inwards, I found friends from other lives. We remembered incidents together, and I felt an extended oneness with the Universe, as though I had at last become a real Member, passing as I did from planet to planet. No fusion, and yet no con-fusion, each in their separate ways working out new infinities of consciousness.

I found Saturn, a most enveloping and strangely lovely planet. We know her mainly for the rings, which to my extended vision stung me into the recognition of a new order of thought.

Everything there worked differently – through a sort of radio-activity is the only way I can describe it. There are no mechanical contrivances whatsoever, all is done through the personal aura drawing from these rings of force. This planet, though physical, is so far removed from the vibration of earth, that one can only explain it as the great linking planet. It's visible to you all; in fact many scientists in the past looked upon it as the Dark Planet, far from the sun and being covered by these rings from receiving the sun's light as we know it. All this is quite true, but the sun's rays are not only the rays of light; they reach us with a hard brilliance, but in Saturn the ray is broken up as by a prism when passing through the rings, and they dissect the vibrations, allowing only those of the higher quality to pass through.

Can we go on with Saturn to-morrow

Tricia

Ma, to go on with my visit to Saturn. The further we got from the sun the higher the vibrations, and inversely, the closer to the sun the lower the vibrations. This explains why Mars is less advanced than we are on earth and Venus infinitely more so. But when we reach Saturn we are on the edge of the great divide between the conscious and the superconscious forces.

I entered Saturn alone within myself, but immediately on entering the rings of Saturn I found separateness was impossible. Individuality was still there, but with our greatly extended auras separateness was quite impossible.

On earth, the majority of your auras are so tightly held into your bodies that no fusion occurs, or at least rarely. But on Saturn auras extend to almost limitless distances from the body, which is of course not a physical body as you know it, but similar, and far more etheric and beautiful.

My first collision with a Saturn aura was rather embarrassing. I slipped into a ring shield and entered the planet's atmosphere to be met by a solid wall of mingled auric light. I didn't understand this at all. It was like a glow of light in the sky over a big earth city, but this was far more beautiful and full of music. I was frankly confused and called for guidance. And immediately a party of the loveliest people came and took charge of me.

They looked like us but they were much taller, and far more radiant and their voices were pure music. We spoke together, because thought is on such a different level that I had to go back to the old esperanto of speech! and how small and unevolved I felt! Just like a new girl. The impact of their auras on me was terrific, they seemed to clap as they met, and I sensed that they were drawing all the discord out of me, I tried to think back over all my late discords and they seemed so small and childish. On glancing up I caught the understanding look from one of the group. A lovely blonde reminding me of one of Botticelli's angels with immense eyes of sparkling colour.

'I know what you are feeling,' she said. 'I was on earth once and had all these experiences, but here all that misery just flows away. The current of God-power is too strong to allow anything petty to stick. It's all a case of circulation. I know the earth beat is very slow, and that is one of the reasons why you are here – to learn to augment it. Once the God-beat is quickened all these discords are pushed

6

aside.' I asked why we couldn't do this more quickly? 'It's going far more quickly that it was when I was on earth,' she told me, 'but you have to teach people the value of Spirit Force, and the non-value of the physical, and it takes a long time to learn it. For instance, you have no need of bodily comfort now, but your love ties are just as easily upset.'

'No, not quite,' I argued, but she was looking into my thought and emotion aura, and she was quite certain that I had held on too tightly to the physical sensation of love. 'Love here is very different. Shall I tell you my story?'

This was just the way I hoped to learn, so we entered each other's auras, and I saw and understood exactly what manner of woman she had been when on earth. Then gradually she passed, after lives as a man and as a woman, not unlike my own, sometimes in the East, and then in the West. Her last had been during the French Revolution when she died in prison, but not from the guillotine. But having been born with everything she lost all, and died of a broken heart. This took her right out of the earth's vibration. Many whom she had loved had preceded her and the rest, both friend and foe, had disillusioned her completely. She was heart-broken that the whole message of the Revolution should have been lost. She was an idealist among the noblesse, and when her eyes were opened she could no longer bear the vibration of earth, and leaving all she went on to Venus. Here she found many old ties, and once again began piecing together some of her earth knowledge.

The Saturn Rings   *Arthur*

Yes, I've been listening to Ronald Fraser and heard all he had to say about the rings round Saturn. I am deeply conscious of a new sense of power coming to us, but I didn't know where it came from. So, off I went, taking Pat with me. It was, of course, Space travel, always a certain effort required from me even now. The condition of the vibes in space change all the time. I'd never been to Saturn, Pat had, and I never realized the great part the Rings played in the planetry energy of Saturn. It's much less dense than earth, and the rings signify her psycho-physical output. Every planet possesses something different, like children in a family; and those furthest from the centre are more original and diverse.

As we entered the region of the rings I found myself growing lighter and melting into them quite easily. This feeling of

7

disintergration is alarming at first, but one soon grows used to it as one withdraws and re-establishes oneself without loss at the end of the exercise! So I willingly let go and entered the life of the rings. I saw Pat was doing the same. They were quite unlike anything I had sensed before. Pat whispered, 'Take all you can and we'll go back to the Moon and examine them.'

On our return, which was swift and easy, we found the vibes contained the embryo of a *new race*. This was exciting. They were only the thought forms of the physical bodies to be created when the right vibe had been found on earth. We then looked at Earth and decided that the normal Earth vibe was not possible; but Earth varies so much, and we were told that a place would be found for these new thought forms in *Siberia*, where the land was quite empty of human life. But, before this could happen the climate must change and become more productive. Another thought form revealed that climate came through the people who possessed higher vibes; so, if these advanced thought forms were allowed to develop in wide empty spaces they could as they developed produce the thought form of embryonic New Races.

BEREAVEMENT: WITH AN ACCOUNT OF A SUICIDE

April 6th 1971   *Rosamond Lehmann*

[*Sally*] Yes, I know what has happened – how 'they' were able to
hide your writing (C.S.'s). I don't know much more, but I see the
state of this friend of my mother's – the result of opening himself in
former lives to the dark forces. In this life he seems to have made
contact with them again while he was abroad. It isn't such a tragedy
as it appears to be. I really think, if he had stayed on earth, he
couldn't have remained sane. Things had gone far beyond his
control. My mother has been a tower of strength to him through
these last months; but he hadn't enough inner strength.

Now he will have a long period of rest in which to restore and free
his ego. His higher self is already free, When he wakes we shall have
his armour of Light all ready to protect him. You have tried to save
him before, Mummy, not only in this life. Now we *must* succeed
before you join him on this plane. Why do you feel the loss of him so
acutely? You have been close in a number of past lives. You were
certainly his mother once; and I think you were lovers once in a far
away Greek life – or lives.

May 21st (returning from Iona)

This is very important. You have been to that darling place, Iona.
Now listen very carefully. Think of D.J. with all the intensity you
can muster. See him actually taking his own God-given life. Feel for
him as a mother; and having assembled all that was good and bad
into one pile of thought, let it all go into the Iona ray – the ray that
cleanses and forgives and searches out the power and the goodness
even in the dross and selfishness which is part of the make-up of us
all.

Poor darling D.J. – you ask if he is happy. Well no – how could he
be? He can't face himself or forgive this last act – and many others.
Does he seek to keep in touch with you? Yes – you are his earth-line.
Whenever he is in a balanced state he yearns for your help. You
have to carry him, and in a later period he will repay. At the moment
he is in a state of semi-consciousness, sometimes wildly miserable,
at others almost in a state of coma. He dreads reaching complete
consciousness. I think he is best left quietly. I suggest – and this

9

comes from advanced teaching – that you work for him morning and evening in the way I described, and for the rest of the day try to put him out of your mind; because thoughts awaken him, and he just can't take it all the time. If he can face himself twice a day that is the most he can do without falling into the Slough of Despond.

May 22nd

Yes, I do agree about poor D.J. (*I had suggested that she should try to awaken in him gratitude for all he had been given on earth*) and I will put it to him that he can begin now, and this will divert his thoughts from himself. Let's not dwell too much on the darker side. Take him into your garden and try to make him laugh again; that would be a real healing treatment.

July 5th

D.J. . . . Well, darling, he is a problem. He is *very* difficult to help. He wants to be his own salvation in his own way; and Christ doesn't work like that. I have talked and talked to him, and I think he likes me because I remind him of you. We have awful arguments, which he generally wins – and then he goes off more desperately depressed than ever. I am *so* sorry for him, but he simply doesn't try to help himself at all. I know he tried before . . . but it's never too late – and he certainly doesn't bother now. When I mentioned your name he paused with a far-away look in his eyes and said; 'That was someone very dear to me in another life.'

Now I find this time-lag most distressing; but I can't see how we can help people who want to be carried all the way. Heaven is a self-service state and no one comes here free or totally carried by a friend. I can't do any more for him. I like him awfully but oh! I do want to smack him sometimes.

July 6th

(*Part of this letter lost. It was about D.J.'s 'Greekness' – his pleasure in physical beauty, his cultivation of the ability to charm and fascinate without getting involved himself.*)
[Sally] How he revelled in being able to draw to himself all these emotions without giving anything of his real self to anyone! He seems to have cultivated a twin personality which reflected a sort of half-false feeling – a feeling without depth. In his last life he deeply regretted this lack. All the beauty and love and passion which he

10

sensed instinctively never seemed to be rooted within; it all came from this twin-genius or spirit; and the real person seems to have floated away, longing in vain to see and feel and know and hear. Even music, which part of him knew he loved, never moved him fundamentally.

No, I can't do anything more for him. All this emptiness has to be experienced, before he can open the doors of perception.

I have learnt to feel so easily what others are feeling that now I sometimes wonder whether I've experienced this or that at first hand – or not! We have so much variety in our generation, whereas the Greeks in those far-off days allowed one thing only – say the magic of a piece of statuary, a line of poetry – to sink so deeply into their inner consciousness that it obliterated all else. There were no cocktail parties to dash off to . . . Besides, they were rustics: they lived much closer to Nature and tuned in effortlessly to the Devic world. D.J. has gathered much from the latter. Can't you see how much he owes to the Devic world? – unheeding, joyous, indifferent, laughter-loving – I feel it all and revel in it myself. But (I think) as an integral part of me – nothing to do with possession by a twin-genius.

July 7th

I am so overjoyed to tell you that I sent out my thoughts of love to D.J. before coming here – and he looked quite different! I could see your love and care thoughts working on him – softening him. That is what he needs – to melt a little and relax. He is so tense. He has steeled himself against accepting what he calls undigested thoughts. He keeps on saying: 'I've not *proved* this or that.' 'Well,' I said, 'don't try. Play it softly and reverse the current. Just experiment with acceptance,' is how I urged him. He laughed and kissed me and said: 'Thank you. I think that was just what I needed.'

So one's efforts have *not* been in vain! I feel so happy. This crisis isn't over; but the worst part *is* over.

September 9th

Now to poor D.J. He has been through a lot and there is still more difficulty ahead but for the moment this is the time of resting. He has suffered – and gone down into the depths of despair, and realised at last that his own feelings don't matter. That is what we all have to learn; and directly we are able to love someone selflessly, and truly say in our hearts: 'I am not important, but by my fortitude

11

I am helping him – or her – to grow into a greater person' – then the test is over. At the moment he is waiting. He has learnt some of the lesson; but now he must awaken a greater power to love; and when he can give himself in that Ray of loving, then the agony will be over. I am getting more and more fond of him – he is such a dear. But still terribly self-centred. Go on sending him love running over; it will be like priming a pump, and will help him to draw an outgoing love from the depths of himself. I have been among many who, like him, have taken their own lives; and I see the diversity of motive is enormous. Some do so from the best of motives – and in a way he was one of these. He felt he was a great drain on and sometimes a torment to his best friends. They were so hopeful of his recovery; while deep in his own heart he felt he was no better. The depression was darker and more clinging. It was a most horrible obsession, and of course he had drawn it upon himself out of sheer curiosity, without making any effort to defend his ego. * The Ego is God and, like the chalice on the altar, must never be desecrated or allowed to meet the evil forces undefended. I don't think you realise how important is this portion of Divinity with which you have been entrusted. Goodness knows *what* you couldn't do with it if you learnt how. I had no idea until I was shown my spirit body and told that this was the Divinity in which I had been clothed. No one knows, no one explains . . . and so our Guardians had to grow a sort of insulating film between us and our real selves. If you wish you can cast this aside at once; but if you do, the entire responsibility is yours. Think this over! We have much to learn together.

* In this context Ego = Higher Self.

September 10th
Now I must tell you that none of our work for D.J. has been wasted. I told him of our meeting and writing, and he woke up quite startlingly and said: 'oh, send her my love! – my new love. I never gave her what she deserved on earth. I was dry as dust, and the milk of human kindness seemed to have gone dry and sunk into the sand of the desert. Now I am beginning to *live*. I can feel the love rays. Tell her that I am really growing'.
That was his message. And then he dropped back to sleep.

12

The following August
I have seen D.J. very often; and I think you can now wipe out all regrets over his manner of passing. He is making good, and it's acting like a spur to force from him great efforts to make up in the lives of those he so definitely hurt – you among them.

December
D.J. and I have been talking over the suicide question; you really ought to publish something about it, because it has a *paralysing* effect.There are some who do it from good motives, such as to free their families – and they are of course exempt. But those who do it, as he did, from depression, allowing the Arch Fiend to gain control – these should be warned, particularly now whem you have so much violence on your plane. Murder and suicide are blood brothers – make this clear. To kill is to range yourself alongside the suicides. And though the murderers have not been through the agony of despair, they have allowed *passionate fury* to enter their finer bodies and cause far greater destruction there than any murderer is able to inflict on his victim.

In the following March came quite a long letter from D.J. himself. He poignantly describes the sense of disintegration he experienced; also his growing awareness of my 'standing firmly between him and complete devastation'. *I repeat this, not complacently but to emphasize what I have learnt, i.e. that one cannot sufficiently stress the importance of directed prayer from friends or healing groups on earth in cases of suicide. They need the strength of our physical "vibes" because of their own low vibratory state. It may even be easier for us on earth to contact them than for discarnate rescuers.*

That letter more or less concluded his story through Cynthia's pen. I felt he was 'safe' and ceased to enquire – though of course I went on sending him 'love and blessings'. But very recently I felt impelled to ask after him again; and this is what Sally wrote:-
. . . Now poor old D.J. Yes, I love him as we all do, and he *is* getting on; but he still can't forgive himself for failing to carry out the mission he undertook: it's a very common feeling among those who opt out, but it leaves a scar, and it has slowed up his development. We all enjoy him, and I think we are a help to him and those like him whom he brings to our group, and by so doing helps them enormously. Such pathetic people – real mixed-up kids as the

Americans say. I use music to calm their awful feelings of recrimination, and they are being given tremendous help from higher spheres . . . He would like to write a word, shall I let him? . . .

'Oh, Ros, how good of you to remember me. I'm not the arrogant self-satisfied person I was. I've lost all that, thank goodness: now I am very humble. I've learnt to creep right out of my personal shell, and can become a chord of music, a coloured ray, or even a line of poetry: it's such a release to become something of a different vibration: but we are warned not to do it too often or we shall become nothing more, and lose our identity. It's one's identity which is so very precious, and it becomes more and more precious as we learn to absorb the awareness of this plane of culture: music, drama, poetry, colour, sound and movement; how I look forward to long, long talks with you . . .'

BARBARA & THE FREEING OF SLAVE SPIRITS IN
THE OLD *CASTLE OF KYRENIA* IN CYPRUS

Letter from Barbara Feb 6th 1955

Cynthia, I'm frightfully interested in these power centres. We, that is our group have been all over the island looking for them, and we have found some beautiful centres, quite different in type, from any that either your father or Olga have seen before. It's quite a new experience for me! We pass over the island at different heights, and try to sense power. I'm a complete novice but Olga and Dick are very good at it. They sensed power here in the Bay, so we all tried in turn to catch a 'sight' of it. It is very like altering the focus of your physical eyes. Once you pick up a tiny glint you know you've got it. I *was* proud to be the first to actually 'see' the green rays coming out of the rock in startling suddeness, it was just like a fountain of colour, and they also have a musical note which I cannot translate because it is so unlike earth music.

The centres on the mountains are nearly all gold and blue, for healing and strength, while those on the coast are used to herald in the new Aquarian age, by mingling the colours blue and green into the auras of the people.

To-day I actually met a Crusader! It was such an event that I could hardly belive my eyes, even though he said he was only a 'phoney' crusader, because he'd incarnated many times since, and had now come back in the guise of a crusader so as to help some of his old slaves who he said were 'stuck here'. (earth bound). I asked if I could help? He seemed dubious, but allowed me to go with him into the Castle.

He took me down among the ruins to the old dungeons, rebuilding the whole place for me on the etheric as we went. It was an enormous, terrifying castle. I asked when he'd been there? He said before Richard of England, and again later. The magnetic pull of Jerusalem had drawn him back through several lives. Once he'd been a Saracen, but he became a Christian and was killed by them within the walls of Jerusalem. Now he is one of the Spirit Guardians of the Holy Sepulchre. (in Jerusalem)

I asked what country he belonged to? which was a silly question! 'I was a Venetian last time, but now I belong to the Main Earth

People; I work for Earth, irrespective of nationality. I carry the Light from the Holy Sepulchre wherever it is needed, sometimes I take it as far as the planets.'

Again I asked 'Why?' – as they are more advanced than we are, why should they need it?

'No, they don't NEED it,' was his reply, 'But they are trying to help us, and their own rays are often too far advanced for our reception.'

I looked closely into the face of this strange man, where suffering seemed to have burnt away much of the vital self. But he was holding himself in reserve.

Suddenly I saw him direct his rays onto the grey shape of a man. The light ran over this spectre putting form and weight into it, then I heard him speaking in a magnificent ringing voice, to some old slave, urging him with great kindness to get up and follow him. The form got up and followed silently. He awakened two others in the same way; and then we left the Castle, and went on to the hillside near the old Monastery. I *was* glad to leave the suffocating damp and darkness of the Castle and breathe the sunshine once more.

The crusader pointed to one of the slaves, and taking one himself he breathed deeply into his mouth. I tried to do the same, it was rather like blowing up an air cushion. Of course I wasn't very successful, and soon passed my slave over to the crusader, and started to help the third. But the third man was not willing to be helped, he pushed me aside and repulsed all our efforts. The other two were quite different. As soon as they had been given enough life, they lay on the grass panting like dogs happy to be again with their old master; but the third slid away from us like a wraith and was back again in the dungeons before we could stop him . . . The crusader merely laughed! . . .

Barbara.

Feb 8th

Letter from Barbara continued

The crusader asked me call him Grafferti, that had been his name as a Venetian, and it was best to use that one inside the Castle where he had last been as a Venetian.

After the third slave had escaped from our good intentions we were both utterly exhausted, and having nothing more to give, we both returned to the upper ether to rest and re-build our powers.

Some days later Grafferti came and invited me to go slave hunting with him again to the Castle. I was willing, and anxious to see and hear more; so away we went, down to the depths of the oldest part of the fortress. I was more adaptable this time and was able to see much more. I was amazed by the number of unawakened 'ghosts' (that is what I am going to call them) still lurking in the lower part of the Castle. Lots of higher mentalities were still earth-bound mainly owing to past deeds of violence and injustice combined with a complete lack of desire to change or to improve their lot. As usual I asked 'Why?' and was told that rescue work had always been going on, but until they were ready for help it was useless.

Grafferti was looking exclusively for slaves, I think he must have been a slave leader (perhaps something like a sergeant).

As we passed the dungeon where the other slaves were found, we suddenly heard his name called, it was the first sound I'd heard inside the walls excepting for the crusader's voice. The cry was uttered in the most doleful wailing tones. We stopped, and Grafferti answered with a bellow of welcome! Whereupon the voice of the wraith seemed to gather strength and out from among the stones of the wall came a limp clammy coldness which I could only just define as being a form. Grafferti seemed puzzled, but accepted the form and infused life into it. Then as before it took shape and weight under his treatment, but this time the form was very tiny, and I realised it must be a woman, who'd been buried or walled up in the Castle. . . .

We awakened two others and left as before, but this time Grafferti chose to enter the cloister of the old Monastery, and leaving the small spirit until the last, we started breathing into the other two. I had barely started, when a scream came from the girl-spirit, and thinking that she was about to escape, I threw out my aura to try and magnetize her to want to stay with us. But she was not trying to run away. As she recovered her strength, the memory of the last moments of her earth-life were so intense that she was re-living her own incarceration! . . . Grafferti luckily knew what to do, and with a few movements of his hand and aura, he put her to sleep on a rock. All this time her form remained shadowy, something which I could only dimly perceive.

The other two slaves responded eagerly, and were soon lapping up the air and sunshine, tremensously pleased to be free again; they were both immensely strong, squarely built men.

17

When Grafferti was satisfied with their progress he turned to the woman, and to my great astonishment we found that during her sleep she had grown into the distinct form of a very beautiful girl. Grafferti roused her, and she woke like a child from sleep looking serene and calm and lovely; but as memory grew within her she shrank into something of her former self. 'Who are you?' asked Grafferti. She struggled to speak, and it seemed as though two people the good and the evil in her were fighting for supremacy. Then she answered with deep resignation. . . 'I am a traitor'. . .

'We have all been traitors at some time or other,' answered the Crusader, 'But now at last you have made it possible for us to reach you— We are Christ's messengers and He wishes us to bear you into the realm where you can grow towards the Highest Heaven.' 'Oh! Can I regain my Queenship?' she asked. 'Yes,' replied Grafferti, 'everyone reaches that through Love and Selflessness'. . . And leaving the two slaves to be treated by other members of our group we took the Ex-Queen back to the ether schools for learning.

Grafferti told me that owing to the fact that the Queen was able to call him she had freed herself from the terrible past which he could read in her aura. I could not see it, but apparently she had betrayed her own kith and kin, and failing to escape had been tortured and then immured into the wall before the Castle fell into the hands of the invaders.

He told me that many of these souls remain fettered owing to the low vibration surrounding them in the actual walls; and that it is only as the world activities and force for GOOD grows more potent that these things can be overcome and the suffering spirits rescued from death.

Barbara

Feb 11th 1955   *Barbara*
I was called again by Grafferti to go with him into the Castle in search of the spirit who had escaped us.

This was quite a different experience. The man had been a slave-driver and extremely cruel. They had all tried to restrain him, but he was equally brutal with himself, and completely fearless. Grafferti told me that he himself had once been saved through the extraordinary heroism of this man, and that now he (Grafferti) must rescue him in return, now that the place of his imprisonment was known. But as our approach had been useless the first time we must go about it quite differently.

There are apparently three great divisions in the strength of spirit suffering, and this man was undergoing the most acute type. I asked 'Why, as he had been so brave?' and was told 'Valour is only of value to the soul when it is rendered consciously, and the spirit of the man measures the cost and accepts the risk in deciding to make the attempt. This man, known as Tula, did neither. His loyalty to his leaders was of a possessive nature; he knew them and trusted them and was secure in mind to follow wherever they led, and if they were in danger or in prison he liberated them instinctively for his own comfort and peace of mind.' So Tula was not a nice piece of work, and to reach his level without losing our grip meant a preparation in magnetism.

First we visited the two neighbouring Monasteries so as to gather the local earth vibrations for *Good* and carry them to the Temple of Mental Power on the etheric plane.

This gathering of vibrations is a real and visible thing to us. The old ruins were entwined with them as with a million giant spiders webs. They did not break but hung from our hands like skeins of the finest silk. We took them to the Great Spirit in charge so that he might weave them into our auras in the form of the 'armour of Light'. Each in turn we stood before him holding the skeins we had gathered while the Lord of the Temple drew them by mental action from our hands and infused them with his higher power, until they were raised to a speed of vibration when they seemed to our eyes to have become like spinning tops of many colours. At this point we had to enter the mental arena and 'sew' them into our auras in much the same manner that Olga taught you to work the Dogtooth veil around your own body.

Once clothed in this way we set off for the castle. I must own I was delighted with my uniform; and the feeling it gave me, as I allowed it to soak into my ether body, was like being born again!

Down we went into the dungeons, lower than I had ever been before. But this time we carried the Light. It's a magical thing to find that you yourself are luminous.

On reaching the place where Grafferti sensed Tula's presence we searched rapidly and soon found him; but he was terrified and loathed the Light. Grafferti spoke to him in the most beautiful ringing tones. I knew he had a wonderful voice, but it was greatly

19

accentuated by his new clothes. In spite of everything Tula was adamant. . .

At this moment one or two other spirits detached themselves and came forward asking for help. Grafferti promised assistance if they would help us with Tula; this promise combined with his magnetic voice drew in a few more until we had a small crowd of volunteers. But Tula became more and more elusive. He sank into the stones of the floor and became identical with the rotting fungus. I can't describe to you the smell of death and decay. . . .

Grafferti on his side was equally determined, and waving to the volunteers to stand back, he called . . . like Christ did to the evil spirits. Grafferti was standing immediately above the loathsome stones, he seemed to shatter the heavy air with his magnetic voice, until suddenly the fungoid fingers dropped dead and the spirit came forth, and instantly enmeshed itself in the aura of his old Master. He had found security, but that was only the first step.

Then followed the supreme effort, to withstand the heavy clogging spirits who had become a dead weight, and were drawing the light out of our auras to a frightening degree. We had promised to help them, and they had now fastened themselves onto our auras. It had been quite different on the previous visits when we used only our own personal magnetism; we could then adjust the flow to suit our strength, but now we had assumed these wonderful electo-magnetic coats without realising that although they could draw the spirit bodies towards us, and at the same time infuse into us a certain amount of power, it still remained for us to provide the motive force to move and use this power.

I must own I felt this was impossible. I was choked by the close oppression of filth and defilement . . . and the horror of it all entered my soul. The cold clammy feeling of death and disease of mind bore down upon me. I called Grafferti, and he replied, but his voice told me that even his great strength was ebbing fast, and that we must call together for help. I tried to call but no sound came from my lips, I was hemmed in on all sides, and had almost given up hope when Grafferti called again. 'Think, do not call . . . See the Light' and suddenly after a few seconds of desperate thought there came a sound like the bells of some old church, softly at first and distant, then growing louder until the sound began to move the rank air of our noisome dungeon.

As the sound grew so the darkness which had been heavy upon us ceased to be a weight pressing down on us. By this time our auras of Light had become utterly obscured by the many clawing shapes which had battened on to us. And now, more welcome even than the sound came the Light, borne by a procession of figures resembling old monks. They came quite slowly, gliding into our vision, growing up in light and form in front of us. Singing and moving in a rhythmic way, while the bells continued to ring, sometimes in high silvery notes, sometimes in deep ringing tones as the rhythm rose and fell.

Then I noticed that between the figures the light was growing more and more intense, until I knew it to be the Greater Light; the Christ Ray which the monks were holding in front of them like a curtain. As they held this flame of Glory it grew until we lost sight of the monks altogether and the form of Christ was made visible to us . . . within the Christ Ray, Christ the Man had sent a tiny fragment of His own greatness to save and protect these spirits who had seldom, if ever, heard His name.

As all this was going on I suddenly realised that my strength was rushing back to me as the spirit parasites dropped away, ceasing to claw at my aura as their only means of escape.

The singing grew in volume until I suddenly realised that the vaulted ceiling of the dungeon had disappeared, and we were all being drawn up and up without seeing or touching the foul walls of this terrible castle. The Christ Ray had become a funnel of Light and suction through which we all escaped into the glowing clarity of the etheric plane; and the terrors of the lowest vaults were cleansed for ever, and light and healing shone throughout all those layers of misery.

The castle had fallen for the last time, and been received back into the Kingdom of Christ . . .

Pro Epilogue

Yes, that is the end of my story. It was a most vivid experience, and I am proud to have been allowed to take part.

This dreadful place is now completely cleared. Our spirit workers have been able to attract all the other inhabitants, and there is now peace and calm, where misery, blindness and cruelty have for so long existed.

Barbara

ANKARA

I am so interested and excited by this place; it was the centre of much turmoil in the old days, conquerors galloped over these plains, and slaves were forced to toil over them in chains, it's full of suffering, effort, greed and power; and now that must all be reversed. The animals are at present taking the vibrational result of all this; but there are a few of the old warriors who have learnt better and come back to help – among them there is this strange figure of Ataturk himself.

I was always very interested in him, as you will remember, so I was delighted to find his vibe yesterday when you walked up to see his tomb. I asked at once how and where was this amazing person, and was shown a glint of his present life. He gave all he had to Turkey and his vision was enough to allow him to escape before he had gone too far. His successor was the person chosen to allow Turkey to rest on her oars for a few years and assimilate all his new ideas.

Ataturk had given Turkey such a jolt, that taken any further she might have disintegrated into communism or gone back to the old tyranny. Dictators run great personal risks when they become demi-gods with no religion to compete for ultimate power, as we saw with Hitler. Ataturk was allowed to pass over at the height of his success, and now, with Turkey and its welfare in his aura, he is working tirelessly among his people, breeding ideas for progress. He knows the strength that comes from empty spaces, he had knowledge of an esoteric type which was born in him, and conflicted with the accepted religion of his youth. I have seen and spoken to him, he is still an aloof figure, rather like Flo, it's strange they should both have served in Turkey. Flo knows and likes him enormously, they are birds of a feather; I talked to Flo about him, and this was her story:

'When Ataturk came over he'd done many things to alter the appalling conditions of his peoples. Of course, had he not been in command at Gallipoli, the British could have ended the war much earlier, but there were deep and curious reasons why this wasn't possible. I was there of course, it was my job to help those who passed over, there were so many English, Australian, New Zealanders and Canadians, and of course many, many Turks. It was through the dying Turks that I learnt about Kemal, and how he had inspired the army.

When the Armistice came, I saw him taking power from the old regime and climbing into the dictatorship. I watched and waited; when he came over I met him. He was terribly disappointed that he'd not accomplished more; I was able to show him the other side of the picture, and explain how he could now work from here, and continue his plan in the etheric. It must all be built into the ether first, he had built in the ether during his early life, and all those plans had been carried out. He was reaching out for others, but they were not yet concrete in the ether, he had over-reached his considered plans, and if you continue with only half-baked ideas, acting on impulse as the occasion seems to demand, then catastrophe waits round the corner. Both Hitler and Mussolini did this.

Kemal is a strange person; in other lives he has been a conqueror, sometimes coming from the East, sometimes defending from the West, nearly always in this part of the world.

He has the vibrations of Tamerlaine, but has now thrown off the war insignia altogether . . . I like Kemal'.

That is her opinion; the next step will be to invite Love to enter his aura; he feels deeply, but there is no love similar to Christ love in his make-up so far. He has nothing to do with his old religion, he recognises God as Power, Health, and well-being as the natural outcome of God-Power, and in this he sees all animals well, and fit, and strong; so tell Lorna Ataturk is with her, and working through all the Turkish people we have met.

My love,

A.

CRETE

After staying in Crete and spending hours exploring the old palace of
KNOSSOS.   *Arthur*

You asked me to comment on the old palace at Knossos; but I
couldn't find anything there. It was all much too old – full of
memories, but even the wraiths had left; and anyway I was much
more interested in the battlefields.

I had never been to Crete, but I'd read a lot about our frightful
disasters there during the war, so I left you and wandered off, trying
to follow the vibes of a modern conqueror.

I soon came upon some arny huts in the etheric, and on stepping
inside in my usual brusque way, I found a sergeant in charge of the
orderly room. He looked up and welcomed me in a semi-army way.
I don't think he saluted, but he got up, and called me 'Sir'. I asked
what he was doing. 'Running the camp, Sir, and keeping the Mess
going for the duration.' I said, 'But the war ended 18 years ago.
What do you mean by the duration?' He laughed and said 'Not that
duration, Sir. We are rather "out-back", but not so far! We are
keeping this place going for the chaps who can't get settled into the
new life. They come over so quickly. Some have gone home –
no-one recognised them. They'd never thought about a future life
and they just didn't know what on earth to do with it. So we decided
to build a camp on army lines, and let them all make a base here
until they found their feet. Many of them enjoyed it all so much we
can't get them to move on; but there's no hurry. No Government
Office insisting upon closing us down, so we go on. They like the
plain, the outdoor life, the history. The open spaces here give them
plenty of chances for development on earth without bumping into
people and getting the cold shoulder all the time. Then as the other
battlefields set up similar bases, some chaps came and visited us and
we got them circulating. I was just one of them myself. I didn't come
over like you, Sir, knowing a lot. I came over very green, and was I
frightened when I found myself out of my body, drifting about? I
hung on to earth, it was all I knew, I wasn't going to lose touch if I
could help it. Hundreds of others felt the same. We were like
drowning men searching for anything we could hold on to that was
familiar. We have wonderful Spirits here at times. They come and

teach us how to move, and think, and use our new powers. It's all very interesting. I'm quite happy to stay on for a bit longer, but I'm beginning to feel a desire to go on, but I've signed on to stay here until the camp closes.'

I thanked him and wandered back to you and Lorna. In the etheric I passed several small parties of men practising etheric athletics and going out to sea doing under-water exploration. I realised that Crete was ideal as a nursery. So perhaps our battlefields and all the misery experienced there wasn't quite in vain.

ANKARA: TEACHING

April 24th 1966   *Arthur*

Oh, this is exciting, I have been here before but so long ago. I was a very primitive person, but I felt a great link with this place, it's one of the biggest natural power centres of the world. Ataturk knew in his inner self, that this was a place of power, which can of course be used in many ways.

On looking back, I see it as a camp for a tribe to which I belonged. I don't know if they were the Hittites; it was pretty crude! Then I came again to Ankara as a European, among the Knights Templar. We seem to have covered much of this country in small parties, generally ending in extermination. I was happy in that sort of life; I can't see more than one or two scenes; I was already trying to heal, I had the rudimentary knowledge and some folk-memory of the Christ power; but we had too much blood on our hands and did not know the way to use the blood vibration.

I have been looking into this lately and I find many surgeons sense that blood has a property beyond the physical, and some of them can use it for healing quite independently of the organ or tissue involved in the operation. When you are trying to help someone through an op., send power to the blood which is released, the spilling of blood releases the power and allows it to flow into the aura: this is why the old anchorites cut themselves to pieces with knives and lashes in order to allow the blood to flow. Christ needed the flow of blood and the soldier was sent to pierce his side – nothing happens by accident.

CHANAK.

May 7th 1966   *Arthur*
I never thought you would take me to the Dardanelles and
Gallipoli. We all came with you on that first act of faith with the car!
And when you reached Chanak, I left, as I always do, to see the
battlefield. Oh my dear, it's the most exciting place, these dreadful
disasters always have another side to them, and this one was very
enlightening to me.

Do you remember that when you took me to Crete I found a
rehabilitation camp going on there (in the etheric) for all the men
who'd been killed fighting in the last war? The same thing on a
larger scale happened at Gallipoli, but of course that has now
reached a further stage. I found the beaches and all the terrain
which must have been soaked with blood and sacrifices now stands
almost uniquely radiant with another vibration altogether.

It may be the same in France, but I have not examined my old
trenches nearly so carefully. Here, this vital element, 'Blood',
united with the ancient vibes to form an archway of radiant power. I
walked into this new condition and asked to meet some who'd
passed over. They came, many of them, some of my old friends,
R.E.s whom I'd known long ago and almost forgotten. 'Hullo, Hill!'
I was greeted with several times, 'What are you doing here?' I told
them, and they told me their stories.

One had died at Suvla so quickly he'd no idea he'd passed over
and stayed with the troop urging them on, until he'd found he
couldn't help them any more. Then he met others in the same plight,
and they carried on, trying to use their mental power to warn those
in the body of oncoming danger and to incite them on.

THE SEMI-PHYSICAL PLANE

I am so glad to be able to write with you again. I have so much to tell you.

I have now met my Twin Soul, it was *such* an experience, both of us being already fairly awakened to life on this plane, and not having met for aeons and aeons before it, made our meeting all the more dramatic, and utterly soul shattering! He is me, and I am him! It's quite glorious. We are the extension of each other, and it is almost worth the long years and lives of separation to gain this when we have both developed enough to realise the completeness of the union.

We have both scampered through our last lives paying off odd debts as I did with my parents and Horace and the boys. I can't begin to tell you what its like, because its like explaining daylight to one in darkness, that's what the earth life feels like to me. All those terrible anguished thoughts, of how to do the right thing, and never knowing. That is absolutely missing here, there is never a moment when we don't know. There is no uncertainty and no suspense.

You ask what we are doing? We are helping to direct the new worlds which are being evolved on different planes. They are all in different states of vibration. We attune ourselves to each as we enter the atmosphere, gather the rays, and plan the power centres, and install the different types of soul who are to live and develop both the world and themselves in the process. Sometimes I train the souls first, and then with their help call into being the world upon which they will live in a semi-physical state. That is the one I am working with now.

Each world has its corresponding twin which works with or alongside it, and for this work Twin Souls like us are used, working together on corresponding planes. This state of the semi-physical is very beautiful. Much of the physical which I still love is to be found and used. Speech, for instance, though no longer necessary, since thought is highly developed. Speech in all its beauty of cadence and rhythm is perhaps at its greatest height on these planes. It is never degraded into just ordinary conversation or slang. It is used only for poetry or prose of a high order, in ritual, or speeches of a poignant or inspiring nature, very different from the uses on dear old earth.

Languages have amalgamated to a certain degree, and many of the finer sounds from other languages long since forgotten are now re-born, and the Power of Words is made manifest. The true meaning of 'Words of Power' has been lost on earth, but here they are in the ascendancy.

I should like to write several times about this plane of Venusian life. Your Father wrote about it once, so it is not entirely new to you.

13th March 1953

Yes, here I am ready to tell you more about these planes. Before you started writing I put into your mind two colours, green and blue. This is the keystone. The earth is on the green plane or ray, we are on the blue. This is your new age into which the earth is now passing. We are on the next step of the ladder of awakening.

In my last letter I called in Venusian life. This means all the planes on that key note, some are invisible, other only partly invisible, while the lowest vibration on this key ray is manifest on Venus. This is the planet on which we start work of this kind directly we leave the earth plane, *if we choose this* for our next set of circumstances. We visit all the planets vibrating to this note with their retinue of higher invisible worlds, all possessing the same or nearly the same nature.

Venus was the one on which I found myself completely attuned. There was no thinking; 'is this what I really like?' It either rebuffs you instantly, or you know at once that you have 'come home'.

My mother brought me here, and together we formed the links which were to bind our work together. She in Iona and I here. Each world has a complete set of connecting lines of force with every other world in their system. So you have links with all the planets, moons and satellites in your universe.

The moment I came to Venus I found myself singing and shouting for pure joy. Something I had longed for instinctively for ages.

I began by learning the method of life and thought. Many old friends joined me, some whom I'd not seen for many lives; but they came and took my hand, and kissed the centre of my forehead where memory is awakened. It was such fun remembering. Suddenly, quite suddenly meeting people with strange faces, and then knowing that I'd been missing them for years and years. With the recognition of each new-old friend I felt myself growing like a tree, putting forth branch after branch with roots to match until I

29

became absolutely part of the intricate fabric of Venusian life.

The joy of action on this plane is beyond description. You know how often we lack the channel through which to express our thoughts and feelings? Here it is all at hand. You long suddenly to ride or swim, to fly, or leap over wide chasms, all power is given to you to do it, and a glorious ecstasy in the 'doing'.

When I'd become accustomed to this freedom of body, and had united the knots of repression to a certain extent, I was trained in the flow of thought, speech, music, painting, still all in action, but related to thought in a new way. When we start writing prose or poetry, we first immerse ourselves in the rays from a certain centre of word thought. This happens to be on a ledge of cliff. The rock rises straight above us and a precipice yawns below! The power passes through us awakening our inner minds. We have to hold ourselves completely receptive and never lose the thread, or the power overcomes us, and we fall from the ledge. Rather tricky to start with; I was so frightened of losing the thread that of course I did, and down I went . . . I couldn't hurt myself, but the feeling of falling is none-the-less terrifying.

This was my first effort, as words were to be one of my channels. I soon learnt the knack of holding the power, but the worst moment came when, having fulfilled the usual period on the ledge, one disengages oneself while still holding the power! Its all great fun and so exciting. We have such amusing incentives to progress, combined with the sense of ecstasy once the contact has been made.

This is all for today

14th March 1953

Yes, here I am again. I've been talking to you about our plane, and you took it in quite easily. I was telling you about life on these semi-physical planes. Communism, in its ideal form, is used and lived here. No one *owns* anything, but it can all be used by anyone so long as it is not misused. For instance, the gardens, of which there are very many. They are called into being partly by thought, partly by action. Digging isn't anything like the labour it is on earth because the soil is dematerialised to a certain degree. The soil is dug, the plant or seed is sown. Water is given in the form of thought. (Thought becomes water when mass thought has been materialised. Does that give you any idea of the vast amount of potential thought lying about upon your planet?) So we don't need to use sprays or hoses, that's all done by *thought*. If anyone tears up or destroys plants out of ill feeling, they lose for a time the power to grow them. After this has happened once or twice, it never happens again.

Vegetables are grown in the same way. When it is done on a large scale a certain number of people attend to so much land, and by their united thought concentrated simultaneously and within a circle. The plants flourish and grow extremely quickly; we don't have to wait for two or three months for our results. Our vegetables are far more diverse and delicious than yours, and since they grow so rapidly we can never suffer from a food shortage. (This is one of the ways in which your food problem will be solved.)

You on earth are due to enter this stage of semi-physical life. Many people are not ready, but they will never be ready if they go stumbling along like this. All these terrible things have happened to your world, in order to rouse and push you forward.

Many are worried over the idea of reincarnation on earth. They need not be, for though they may, and probably will return here, it will be to a new earth, and a new era of cosmic life. All these things now happening to you are the embryo of the life to come.

We are working upon twin planes which, when fully developed, will take their place one on each side of the earth and by their rays focused upon Earth will call forth new and unknown elements.

Ah! you say, but this is all in the far future. But I can only tell you that Earth is lagging behind, and holding up the universe! So evolution must go on, and swiftly.

I want you to understand all this because we want the knowledge of it to be within the ether. It helps the manifestation, and gives you something to work towards.

Now, to go back to describing our conditions. We have a central Government of which I am a member, in fact I think you would call me Minister of Agriculture. We have cities, but they can be created overnight and folded away into the atmosphere by day, if we wish. You can't imagine how convenient this is! There can never be any squabble between me and the Town Planning Officer. If I need an extra area for food, I have it by day, and they have it by night. We grow all we need in the hours of daylight, and when night falls, we and all creation, sleep . . .

There is very little crime on this plane. Crime comes through mistakes made and exasperation over the manipulation of thought.

31

But everyone registers a great and immediate discomfort of wrong thinking. So it happens very rarely.

We have the most glorious forests. I think they are one of our greatest beauties, and in them most of our scientific work is done. The trees are far more help than any University buildings have ever been. They hold the physical power and we tap them for it in almost the same way that you still tap the rubber trees.

My father is in charge of the forests, and you can imagine how happy he is, Mother is often with him, but, as you know, her chief work lies at Iona. That is a spiritual centre far exceeding the normal power on this planet, but it passes through our plane and so on to the spirit planes, giving us just that amount of boost to keep us from settling down contentedly in our own lovely rut. Which is so perfect that I for one am ready to work here for many aeons to come.

15th March 1953
Cynthia, can we go on? I don't want to lose contact or rhythm.

Today we will talk about art. Yesterday I told you a little about government but that is so much governed in its turn by art I must pause and go into it now.

Unlike the earth plane, where art takes a poor second place in the affairs and history of the nation, here it is one of the most moving forces. We cannot enforce any rule without the assistance of art first to demonstrate the need. No rule is imposed without a unanimous acceptance. There are no laws, only rules. For instance, the acceptance of the rule of universal work is illustrated first in music, then in painting, and lastly in prose. You may think that an odd way to do it. The music brings the theme, the painting the illustration, and the prose brings them both to a definite point. So our leaders are also artists, musicians, painters and writers. (Ballet has also vast scope for illustration and comes into the category of the artist.) All these methods are used to inspire *ecstasy* which is almost unknown to you, it is the immediate touch of God.

On the Spirit planes the touch is constant, here it is only intermittent, we have not yet grown the finer body which can hold the constant ecstasy of the God Touch, it would destroy our bodies and burn them. So the contact here is like a make-and-break in electricity. It happens all the time. The vital thing is only to work for development during a 'make' period and never in the 'break' period.

32

You have this to a very much lesser degree on earth, and you can understand what I mean.

The painter here does not mix his paints . . . he just paints, and the colour flows from his brush as his thoughts catch the inspiration from the God Touch. We do not need many rules, but we are for ever probing in order to learn how to use the laws connecting us with the higher powers as they come within our reach.

16th March 1953
I am so sorry to have worried you when you had the 'time panic'! How well I remember it.

We spoke last time about art being the active inspirational motive behind all action, and the intermittent contact between ourselves and the spirit spheres. At first this God Touch is terrific, and one can only hold it for a very short time and then relapse back into the physical. But as we grow accustomed, we are able to hold it for longer and longer intervals, and as we gain this power we are given increasingly responsible work in the government of this plane, until we reach the stage of being able to leave the plane completely, for one of pure spirit. I have actually reached this stage – quite a low level of spirit, you know. I am entirely free of the physical, but I have chosen to remain and do this work.

So we go from planet to planet as they are called into existence, helping them to evolve. In this way everyone evolving on the semi-physical plane has the experience of government responsibility. If they are specialists in art, science, literature or ballet they become leaders in those subjects instead. No one earns promotion without the ability to hold pure spirit. I wonder what your government would feel like if that rule were imposed.

Sex is still with us but much of its grossness has been shed. Child-birth is a joy, and not agony any more. Semi-physical children are the most delightful creatures, real Will o' the Wisps, tireless sparks of happy energy. This is the plane of perfection in childhood. Those who come here as children having reached this stage of development, are generally the still-born babies from your plane, or children who have died in infancy. I found one of mine here, a most charming boy. He has grown into a man, and he welcomed me like an extension of Hugh, and made me feel so much at home. The impish pranks they play here put all the earth children's effort to scorn. They have such deft brains and light etheric bodies. Keeping discipline among the unruly young is quite another matter, and has all to be done through mind influence. Many psychoanalysts come here to find the answer to their theories. We work on the mind, never on the body. The child is given full freedom of body, to do what it likes, when it likes, and how it likes, and if anything it does is definitely wrong, great distaste for it is placed in the mind. For instance, two small imps of my acquaintance decided they wanted to be 'grown up' and 'married'; so they started to build a house. This is done by half by thought and half by hand, and of course, as on earth, it was outside their power, but they made a sort of wigwam and were prepared to live in it. Nothing was done to stop them. There are no climatic laws that make it necessary to live indoors, so they moved into their house, and became quite independent. Food is grown easily and quickly, so this was no barrier. They said they'd had enough teaching, and were not going back to the Circles, as schools are called. No notice was taken, so they had their way, slightly missing the companionship of all others, and not feeling quite as 'grown up' as they'd intended. 'I know what it is,' said the boy, 'to be really grown up we must have children.' But their bodies had not reached the age of puberty, so could not respond and the whole thing collapsed, and they went gladly back to school, almost as if nothing had happened.

You can't think how easy it is when these laws are applied. All surly tempers and moods disappear. So many of your troubles, both juvenile and mature are due to frustration, and to that awful sense of ownership. Here we produce nearly all we want out of the ether; clothes, for instance, can be entirely etheric and many kinds of food, so by a natural law we cease to want them.

The real foods for the physical part of the body are still grown as I explained. They are all fruits and vegetables; and for the sake of Patricia tell her that no cooking is done on this plane! But we do have the most lovely banquets. You can't imagine the beauty and variety of the foods, often accompanied by a rich supply of etheric sweets and wine. They can also be made physically, but the etheric are even more delicious.

17th March 1953
Let's go on from where we left off yesterday.

I want to tell you about taste and the desire for food. This is a great stumbling block for your bodies on earth, and we hear so many voices saying, 'eat this, eat that, drink so and so, or never drink anything! Only eat to live, and never to enjoy'. And so on. What a muddle! The truth is that during a time of greed the desire for food has entered the astral and is now reflected through to the physical. Now, when your physical body cries out 'no more please', your astral remains unsatisfied, and until you get your astral out of this habit it will continue to produce the glutton and the drunkard.

When people come here, they can satisfy the astral on the astral plane, with the food which satisfies the desire, without overloading the physical body; and when an unnatural desire can be satisfied it automatically ceases to exist.

So much for food. Let us now talk about Life, just ordinary life, how we live and what we do.

A new arrival here sleeps a lot and is encouraged to get all the weariness out of him. We don't sleep in houses or on beds unless we want to, but new arrivals generally feel more at home in them. Then, as they learn to move about, the idea of food, what shall we eat and so on becomes urgent! Many are born on the semi-physical plane as children, and sleep and food are natural needs.

There is no money here, and no barter, for there is nothing to exchange excepting places to live, and in different kinds of work. Some want to change to the sea, others, to the mountains, one turns from science to art and so on. There is a constant flow of change enabling most people to go through all the different branches, and experience all the different climates before leaving the plane.

There is no death or warfare. There is no national feeling. Colour is not the same barrier, your skin re-acts according to the particular climate where you work, it darkens in the tropics and becomes paler again in the cooler climes. The constant change eliminates race and nationality. Our bodies are fine enough to suffer very little from illness, cold or heat. Such clothes as we need are mostly etheric, that is, produced by personal thought, but there are still some made from a vegetable texture, which is half physical. But all the 'exquisites' in dress are clothed entirely in the etheric. You can produce anything by thought; after practice this can be done almost immediately. One delightful thing about etheric gowns is that they always fit superbly, because they take the exact mould of the body from the mind through which the thought was emitted. Many of the 'exquisites' here live in houses, mostly etheric houses of fantastic beauty. They are sometimes built of stone or wood, Daddy is not very keen to let his precious trees be used in this manner, but they do all the same.

As people grow up the need for sleep becomes less. They dance and are gay, have sports and competitions, fall in love and marry; no question as to whether they have enough money to provide for a wife and family. It's all to hand, and life goes on and on until they have reached the stage of holding the God Touch indefinitely. Then, and then only, are we ready to leave this lovely planet.

There is no sadness of parting, but a great celebration of happiness on the attainment of further freedom. 'Death' to them (as to you) means liberation. They can return, as we can to you but they are seen and heard and can enjoy full converse with this plane, even when they are in a pure spirit body.

The conversion of your plane of the wholly physical to this stage has to grow slowly, but it has already begun. From the moment when the unseen forces were discovered, the physical era began to recede. Electricity, wireless, television and all the myriad other rays used or only apprehended by your scientists were the beginning of this new age.

Glastonbury and Iona, linking up with all the smaller power centres are now being stimulated to urge this forward. Alice Bailey who knew all these things once said, 'In fifty years time, death as you know it will have passed away' and that was spoken twenty years ago!

Each day is bringing you nearer to the Land of Heart's desire. It will extinguish discontent like water putting out a fire, but like a fire it will hiss and snarl at losing its power over mankind, and it will take time before full understanding can penetrate. You will have to be very patient until the power of sight becomes universal. You will first apprehend – rather like you do now – then, and not far hence, you will start to 'see'. This will be the cleansing of all your doubts, the end of death and despair, and of blind suffering, and of fighting on without hope or knowledge. You will pass the portals of the New Age without knowing that they have been reached. And when you enter the Palace of the King, you will accept the inheritance and enter the Royal House of Spiritual Awareness, to which we are all drawn by the Great Almighty Father.

TEACHING

You are now at such a vital stage in the life of your planet, I wish some times that I were still in the body, knowing what I do now, but I don't expect I could waken people up any easier. How I long to give you an idea of the vastness and the approachability of all these marvellous forces. You are like bunches of wire wrapt up and insulated to such a degree that very little or nothing can come through. But I am here to give you hope, if not certainty, that the sum total of Good in the world so far exceeds the less good that the end is easily foreseen. I am longing to show you how to use your new body, and listen to the exciting new word patterns coming from not only your planet but from the furthest reaches of the universe.

I learnt slowly to illuminate distance. Space and distance, which to you are infinite, can be easily traversed by the strength of thought. This came home to me after I had won my way through the gravitational circle and become a true Etheric. Once you have cast off all your ordinary human vibes you enter another zone of thinking and seeing and our bodies cease to have form and become sets of vibrations with a far heightened awareness and an ability to accept the new values which bombard us. I am for ever trying to sift what to me is the true path, while to others a different path may well be chosen. I have found the deepest parts of your ocean were the most exciting places from which to relay prayer. Does that amaze you? We have the most lovely ray temples in the depths of the sea where no human has ever penetrated.

When I enter these planes I get the most enormous awareness of utterly super-etheric Beings, whose minds are so far beyond our normal thought that I am dumb with excitement. One cannot absorb or understand these high entities but they give us all a real BOOST, and when I look back upon the very low boost of many of my earth life conditions I am ashamed to be seeing and feeling so much that I am totally unable to convey to you; but all the time your aura is expanding and the colour is becoming more active. You can change your mood of despondancy merely by substituting a colour and seeing it glowing all around you. Some friends of mine were investigating this one day and they went into a churchyard and extracted two girls from a new release into spirit and they asked me how they reacted. They were overpowered by JOY for getting free from the body: this showed me that cremation is the quick and natural way to leave. So if you have any desire to lie snugly in your coffin in an earth grave, 'forget it Sister' as one of the newly dead said to me. I think a lot of people think that this is not the way, but from my own experience I say YES to cremation.

I pass from age to age of the different soul bodies; they are all so distinct and I feel that something can be learnt and given to everyone I meet. This feeling gives one the great sense of unity which was never felt on Earth. You will enjoy the great freedom here, but why wait? Try to imagine yourself weightless, tireless, disease-free and to see others the same. We need to prepare the conditions for the next plane before we reach it, and so why not begin now?

I have so much to give you: when you are tired throw yourself down on the bed and let me enfold you with my love as with two great wings, and draw from me this sense of awareness of the next world. This will ease your passing and your first spasms of uncertainty.

Arthur

CASSINO

April 1965   *Joe*
I want to write about Cassino because it interested me so much. I find the whole place intersected by the past ages and inhabitants as no other that I have ever seen. It has a far greater future than its dramatic past. Like Churchill, events were formed to cleanse and destroy this place so that it should grow into something outside a purely doctrinal centre. Hence the reason why the armies of many different races gave their lives in protecting and attacking it. They have all helped in some way. Many were agnostics, some belonged to other creeds who now extend their influence outside and beyond Roman Catholic thought into the infinite. There were some very deeply scientific minds among them who still live in the precincts.

I had a long talk to an R.E. who had been there on and off and eventually died of wounds in hospital. He was captured by the immensity of the place, the isolation of the stronghold; it took hold of his imagination, and our talk went something like this:

A.F.S. How long were you in the attack on Cassino?

R.E. Oh, I was preparing for it, making the plans for disrupting the whole place, but I felt as though I was working at something too big; mere man-made explosives couldn't do the trick.

After I came over, I found myself still thinking how it could be done, and wandering up and down the mountainside. I hadn't realised then that I was 'dead', so I became rather short and rude if anyone got in my way, and I found myself passing through them in a most uncanny manner. I thought at first that they were queer, and then I began wondering if I was the queer one! And a sense of isolation closed in on me. I couldn't remember where H.Q was, or who were on my staff. My A.D.C. had been killed, but I knew he was in the offing, and when I caught sight of him I made him come and discuss the position; and together we came to the unpleasant conclusion that we were 'dead'.

I was terribly disappointed. I'd begun to grasp the situation, I had a plan in my head, but now it was all shattered. But the boy was far more sensible. He said, 'Well, Sir, we may be dead in our bodies, but we are alive in our minds and we can move and see and plan more easily; why not go right up to the monastery and have a look-see all round. They can't see us or hurt us now; it'll be a huge joke.' I didn't like the way he put it, but I saw his point: and so we went together. It was quite easy. We slipped or floated up the mountain. No tortuous route, no exertion in climbing. And then we were there, among the defenders. Tough German troops on the 'ring' and the monks still inside. I wasn't a member of any church, so I felt quite outside the religious sense of the place.

I asked if the Germans were using Cassino.

R.E.   Not physically, but they were getting all the information, photographs etc., via the monks. It was too much to ask them not to collaborate in some way. The German Commander asked the Abbot to sign a paper saying that no German had entered the Monastery, but that was only the letter, not the spirit, of truth, and the rest the Abbot was ready to overlook. Whether it was wrong to bomb the Monastery, I do not know. But it *had* to be destroyed in order to be born again on a fresh Foundation, and fire had to cleanse it.

We were at the fall of Cassino, and saw the Polish soldiers advance. We met the Polish dead and carried them up to the summit, so they all died knowing that they, every one of them personally, had *won*. It was a great day of unfoldment. The Germans whom we met and also helped knew it was the virtual end of the campaign. They were astounded when we showed them the vision of the new Cassino on the etheric which will now enfold the physical.

On the day of retreat and advance we held a ritual of welcome on the summit in which all who'd fought at Cassino took part. Those who'd gone over at the beginning and throughout the long drawn out attack were among them. Many of them were advanced souls and they formed a brotherhood with all the rest of the besiegers. It was an exciting end to a long story of endeavour.

PREPARING FOR DEATH

12th February 1971   *Joe*
Death has been made into such a bogey that it is only through
suffering and discomfort that we are persuaded to let go and
co-operate with death. The body fights to retain life on any terms as
long as it can; this is the inborn instinct of the body-brain. So we
have to re-educate it to accept the hour of passing, the hour when
the body-brain will relinquish its power over the body it knows,
willingly, without waiting for the body to be wrenched away from it
through pain or disease.

This teaching is going through on several different waves towards
body consciousness, and you will find more and more people just
die in their tracks, which is the ideal way of leaving. But we are all so
closely knit together it is often very hard to drag the Spirit-body
free. I told you that I had experienced a strange feeling of a power
that seemed to be drawing me out of my body during the last few
days of my illness. I was so hopelessly ill, and I knew it, that I
welcomed this inrush of new life and let go very willingly. That was
why I did not linger as many others who long to hold on to life.

You must all realise now that you've joined the 'club'. The OAPs
that the passing cannot be very long delayed, and be ready to
receive the power which draws you quite painlessly out of your
body. It's the most beautiful and glorious thing. I see so many are
prolonging life quite unnecessarily. They have finished their task,
the mission is ended. If you do this, giving up the reins, as it were, to
the Great Creator, and expressing your readiness, then life is
withdrawn so gently and lovingly, and the dossier of your earth
effort is closed.

All my love,
Joe

TWO DIFFERENT WAYS OF PASSING OVER

Joe

I woke up finding that instead of never waking up again I was more alive than ever. The discords within me were so strong that I gave up for a second time, and said, 'you take over, I can't fight any more,' but before doing so I had one last moment of sense to throw out a despairing cry to my mother who had passed over some years previously, and she came and salvaged me.

First she just talked to me quietly. I was so delighted to hear her voice that I began to take heart. She explained that I must throw off the discords that were like discoloured patches on my etheric body. She treated them at once, and I saw the instant result. Then she urged me to move. I couldn't. She insisted. I sat up, and very shakily got to my feet, but I fell again and she caught me and let me rest for a while. Then it began again, move, walk, think, eat, drink and grow. Throw off all regrets and discords. 'You are starting a new life with a clean sheet.' Slowly, slowly I gained control over my new body until I could move and think and become like other etherics, and I learned that all the discolour was due to my having allowed depression to enter and take hold of my finer body, and when I had only the finer body to use I was absolutely sunk. So my advice is 'Cultivate your awareness of this other body and make it work for you. Let it become part of all that is best in you, throw out all grudges that take root so easily and become cloying anchors to your advancement.'

Here is another example of what happens when you have used the other body before leaving the physical.

20th January 1975

'I came over almost consciously; in fact I did not know when one life ended and the other began. I had lived alone and been unable to walk far, and I needed passionately to know how my family were getting on miles away. So, I thought of them most lovingly as a grandmother should, and gradually a response came to me, often questing for a reply, or even a decision. What shall I do? Naturally I could not and should not attempt to answer these questions, so I placed them upon the Christ level, and asked that a reply should be sent. In several cases this proved to be possible and successful. The main proof to me was that by using one's finer body as an extended telephone one could receive, and by opening the communication to reception on another line of perception one could in some minute way tap the All-Knowing Spirit.

This gave me, an old infirm woman, a great sense of expansion and growth, and when I passed over I had an immediate contact with everyone I had ever known and loved.'

So the infirmity of my body turned my escaping thought-body into a telephone exchange on a high level.

JOE'S PAST LIFE ON IONA

My next vision was of Iona. Here I became somehow in charge of the boat or boats owned by the monks. It was a very simple life and I suppose a hard life, but I was happy and secure.

I remember being sent away with a great leader through the islands. It might have been St.Columba, but I don't think so. He was able to use several rays of thought power, and I was not always necessary to him for transportation. Sometimes he seemed to use levitation entirely, but at others he came to me for help, and we sailed together. I have only broken memories of these cruises as we battled with the sea in a very small roughly made boat. But I know that I never feared making harbour if he was with me, nor was there one moment's boredom with this man on board. He was gay and strong and full of laughter, and also full of interest; I knew he was expounding things which I couldn't understand then, but they stayed in my subconscious and I am gradually recalling them now.

He was always stressing that Power was deathless, and that something of great power had been created in the beginning of the world in Iona. He said we were very lucky to have made contact with this power, and it would always flow through us in the form of a magnetic current. Then as he spoke he would suddenly say 'Ah, we've hit one now, I shall not need your help to-day,' and with that he was lifted out of the boat into the air and away towards the island of his destination, while we sailed slowly in his wake.

THE SUN

Joe

The sun is a most mystifying part of our universe and I am not sure, even now, whether I am remembering a physical or an etheric sun. But what happened to me was not alighting upon a world of molten rock or metal, as I had been led to expect on earth, but on an extremely beautiful planet which was encompassed by a glowing atmosphere of fire.

How it became in that state, or whether it was reflected from elsewhere I do not yet know. But it was only the atmosphere that blazed and gave light of surpassing beauty to the land beneath.

I can't describe it. It was completely outside speech.

I've met the young SUN people as well as those from other planets, and so far I have not penetrated to the centre of creation, and as each step is shown and understood, so I feel I must go on to the next.

First we think of London as a great capital, and New York, and then of the Earth going round the Sun, and now the SUN is going where?

I have not got to the end of that question, but we are sure the further we go there is always another step ahead. It is a place teeming with surprises, this great universe.

I wonder if we shall ever grow big enough to grasp it all?

But that doesn't matter. The important thing is the enjoyment of it and the LOVE that keeps the machine moving.

I am tremendously interested that Russia has been allowed to enter the race, almost lacking in the Love Ray, but full of desire to succeed.

You are now beginning to grow into the citizenship of the sky. Isn't that an exciting moment?

I think all our immediate neighbours – Venus, Mars, Jupiter, Uranus and so on, have always known and enjoyed each other, but not Earth.

SAUCERS

I met your brother-in-law George the other day. He is just as interested as I am in the new movements all over the world: Africa seems to be his baby while Russia and the East are mine. He was full of ideas about this flying saucer *force coming to intervene, but needing an invitation* from earth before they could step in. I have not dealt with this at all, I was fascinated to hear that if and when they come they would bring a new set of ethics with them; that their bodies are more or less allergic to disease, and that the very presence of so much life force will improve the physical health on earth and make clear untired thinking possible.

That chap Adamski is working with them and has always insisted that a world crippled by illness and weariness could never prosper, so the first thing is health, the second is to eliminate selfishness in just the same way that you would dishonesty. Prosperity and health would draw this nearer to us and then dispel these fatuous ideas of ambition and keeping up with the Joneses. In fact all the young who are opting out of the 'rat race' are giving their consent to the saucer people.

I asked if it would be an invasion? He said no, nothing so dramatic. Many would just appear among us, living our sort of lives but setting a new formidable standard, because they had found happiness within themselves that we as a race have not. We are not at ease within ourselves.

George is going to introduce me to some of these other people, who, though in physical, are far enough advanced to see and communicate with us. It was all very startling and exciting. Please remember this and be ready to welcome the stranger with a new rate of values into your home! It's a most exciting time of transition both for you and for us.

George told me how he'd met some of these new people in the Sahara. They had landed unseen and made a contact with many of us who were in the etheric but more or less new arrivals. He was led to them by the waves of force emanating from the machines. They have the power to draw all those who really wish, and reach out in thought towards, a better understanding with the forces of Light.

46

They look like us, but they are much more dynamic and full of vitality. The ones he met, men and women, fair with blue eyes and the most hypnotic light in their eyes, and their shining heads of hair were almost like an aura of gold around them. You felt their composure and complete happiness; that was the only way he could use to describe the sensation they gave him. At once he said, 'I felt lifted up into another way of thinking and everything about them seemed to glow, not in a dazzling, but in a magnetic way in which one almost sensed Divinity.'

I asked what happened next. He said, 'They gave us all instructions on how to prepare areas in which they could make a base. The deserts were obvious places for several reasons, including the sunshine on which they depended for food. They seemed to live on a strange vegetable diet which fertilised and grew very rapidly in the sunshine. He said to one of them, 'You look like the Children of the Sun.' They answered, 'That is our mission.'

I was tremendously impressed by all they told us and it has already started in a small way in America, where young people have gone out into the wilds to produce food and live simply. He said it would begin there, but many other places would be colonised, Russia, Africa, China among them; and Britain was not to be left out. Our great magnetic centres were to be points of contact. He wants to write with you on this subject when you are on Iona.

AUTHOR OF 'FLYING SAUCERS HAVE LANDED'

Feb 10th 1967   *Patricia and Adamski*
Ma here we are, I've been having great fun with Adamski; I've brought him here, he was not too keen to come at first, but he was on earth working in California among the astronomers, and quite glad to leave their shut-in minds. He has been to Joderell Bank and finds our people much more open to suggestion. He says we need to get more mind training, before a real landing is made. He keeps on saying, 'If only they could get off the ground themselves and use the magnetic currents. If they could reach that state of development it would be far easier to impress them with our saucer-craft.' He says it will come soon and you will find yourself floating just off the ground. Think of this and try it, you'll soon begin to get the flying habit, but won't it be amusing? I can see a lot of very funny things happening at first.

Adamski 'Thank you, yes, I could tell you a lot of interesting facts about the saucers, but you want to contact them and to do that YOU must know within yourself that this is possible and attain to an air-borne-consciousness. Unless you get this, the knowledge that we can help the saucers to bring to you, will only be interesting phenomena without any scientific link with your state of knowledge and development. I KNEW so certainly that saucers were coming from space that my faith gave wings to my sight and hearing and to my believing. I am convinced that the earth will be changed by the saucer landings.

It is time that you got away from the surface right now, you are doing yourselves no good staying on the surface or by flying in planes; but you can by your own links with us in this form of thought be able to leave the solid ground and move in the lower ether by your own volition.

I know you call me a crank, and so I am. But you must get started out of this earth rut. Don't you see how much you have trodden into the poor old earth? Now is the time to float over it, to cease from illness and to get cracking on another line of thought. Oh, I like that fellow at Joderell Bank, we think along side each other, but he must go further and further; I see you are all hampered by seldom having perfect health. This means you are only allowing a small intake of light into your bodies . . . When I say light I mean this God Fabric which gives and grows and puffs us up like balloons, and unless you can be filled by this Spirit of God you are ill and heavy in thought and consciousness. It's this last thing that gets me thinking so hard, I just can't figure out how your brains can be speeded up to work faster unless you are healed of all infirmities, great and small; or how to float your mind away from your body. Do you get me? Your mind just can't operate inside your skull, it never could. You must send it out and out into your finer body. . . Oh yes, you can do this, or I would not be writing it.

Now I've got a lot more I'd like to say, can we do this again? I am working on health sheaths and the force that will carry you off the ground; not far to start with but out of contact with the soil without any metallic instrument between you and the lower ether. I want you to wash your auras in the glorious lower ether and get cracking on some of these more exciting lines of thought and action . . . and mind you, they are all within your power.

Adamski

This is an experience at Christmas written by Canon Shepherd who translated several of Rudolf Steiner's books

Dec 26th 1968
My dear Cynthia,
I have had the most exciting, revealing and enlightening Christmas that you could ever imagine in your wildest dreams. I have been completely dissected, divinely torn to bits, and in spite of the mental agony at times, it was all immensely satisfying, and I could feel myself achieving something beyond thought.

I will begin at the beginning. We knew from Pat's letter exactly what to expect, and how to prepare for this Coming of Divinity, but one can never know until it happens to oneself, personally, how great and distorting and finally re-creating this experience can be. It is in a sense what we call the second death – each year we enter into this area of greater Divinity, just as Pat descibed, rising up and up and losing sight of everything, and feeling alone in the vast expanse of Eternity. This is frightening. I longed to call but dared not, and the thinning of my own self, my very person on this plane became almost dismembered. I have hands and feet, shoulders and legs, but they seemed to float away in this weightless, timeless region. Only my brain, my thinking, feeling centre, remained mine. I waited with a certain discarnate horror for the next dismemberment, but it never came. With silence I began to sense, not exactly a sound, but a rhythm, beating upon my brain, inside my head, building, creating and extending the power of thought and feeling; and then into my vision came the blinding sense of the immense Presence of Christ. Presence does not explain the wonderful nearness of this Divinity that was surging around me and inside me. For a moment I was actually a part of the Divinity and then my power to register this great Presence overcame me and I slipped back into the shell which I knew and understood.

There was no sense of loss and when I relinquished the participation with Divinity, only a great swelling of pride that in a small, infinitesimal way my Sonship had been established.

This is all I can write today, but I have much more to tell you later.
My love to you all everywhere.
Arthur Shepherd

Alexias,* How wonderful to be near you again.

I have become a much simpler person, having dropped all the intricacies of the individual I became in earth life. But it is different when you take on a whole number of other lives; and their residue is clogging – although at the same time it aids every step in thought you take. Fortunately I was able, in my last days, to differentiate between my various selves and even confer with them. It was fun! Think this over. You have your Greek and Egyptian priestess shells still close to you. Draw them in separately and learn what they have to give. It's most instructive, most intriguing – and at times very amusing.

For instance I was an astrologer-alchemist, philosopher, writer and so on. Some of these cancel each other out if they meet in opposition; but taken as a whole they can enrich your faculties enormously. I was often rather frightened that one or the other would take charge to the elimination of the rest. So there was a war going on within me most of the time which made me aloof and aggressive. I don't think you have these warring entities; but you have many faculties developed in Greece, Rome and Egypt that would be of value. I am meeting all kinds of interesting people of all ages. I learn. I read the Akashic records. I go off into the vast areas of uninhabited parts of the world and have found power and thought centres with the rocks and the trees – particularly the rivers. You will be delighted with these centres. They are peopled by writers, thinkers, artists and scientists from all ages: very large numbers are Greek. They seem nearer to our thinking than the rest. Egypt is too far off: Rome too military: and France – well, France is always with us, bless her. She has mothered me through several difficult but very interesting lives – one at the court of Louis XIV. How I loved and hated it all. But now I must say goodbye, Alexias. We met not so very long ago in that rich France of my letters.

But here is Sally looking very stern and fully determined that I have had my say. Goodbye for the present – and my endless love and enjoyment of you – you personally, your writing and your laughter.

* The name he gave me. R. L.

When I met my G.S. I was, as you know, feeling my way among new truths. I hadn't lived for very long (on earth) so my score of good and evil in my last life was not a long one. In this sense we who pass on young can assimilate the G.S. far easier than someone like Joe who had led an intense life full of interest and action – with a million different influences falling in all directions.

I *saw* my G.S. and thought it was a reflection and was quite shocked when it spoke to me! We held a curious conversation during which I saw the enormous advantages of entering into partnership with this other Self. I think, in youth we feel the drag and the push of different parts of us, and know that we are the battleground for so many instincts; so that when you come over young a separate entity from yourself, who is still a part of yourself, is not so strange. But after a long life these instincts have become crystallised into a sort of organised whole; and to break up that conglomoration of selves in order to admit a new and completely non-selfish You must be very painful. In my own case I was simply transfigured with joy! At the time I was rather lost and miserable, and saw dimly that here was a whole determined Me – a Me whom I knew I could trust and look up to and lean on. That was the personal side. Then came the interest of going into all the little pieces I had acquired as fit to be kept from so many other lives. It reminded me of that TV programme This is Your Life! And as each life appeared on the screen of memory those I'd loved and hated came into being before me – and I embraced them all. This was rather hard in some cases: but my G.S. stood by and said: You must, *must* pour out the love of complete forgiveness. After one or two half-hearted efforts I managed it quite easily. The love stress is so strong here. I was just impersonally pouring out Divine Love to make a bridge between us, which is what we must all do with our enemies. Be quite impersonal.) Just gather up the love stream as you would any other building material, as a *bridging reality,* and walk over it; and you will find the enemy is no longer at your gates but resident in your heart.

This picking up of all the threads of past lives goes on and on: I haven't nearly finished my researches. I've had all kinds of lives. We have all been slaves: and those lives have perhaps been among the most fruitful. *Stress this.*

I was a painter in Florence long ago – not distinquished – but I knew and rubbed shoulders with Botticelli and many others of that date; and I lived and loved that artist vibe in Florence. It was a hard life; hunger and disease were always at our doors. I think I eventually died of plague; but before doing so I'd learnt something of the skill of the artist, and that skill becomes mine again when I enter the vibration of the period. It's an enormous asset having been given a good education and having formed pictures in my mind of how one lived and worked in those days. From my schoolroom memories it sounded idyllic! but in real life I see it was a struggle on a far larger scale than anything we know now.

I was shown the horrid little room where I lived and worked; and the extraordinary interest taken by everyone in drawing and sketching. They watched one in the street or the tavern until one's hand shook with nerves and debility: because one was very open to suggestion from the crowd and very tense. The crowd's appreciation stimulated one's capacity to draw and paint. I can hear my old Master saying 'Don't paint alone. Go out and work with people; they will bring out the power in you – if you have it. If you can't work with people round you you are no artist.' So out I went in the freezing cold, to the tavern if I had any money. If not I pleased the crowd and they would stand me a drink of this queer sour wine.

It's fascinating re-living a life, or part of it. It's very painful in parts, seeing the people one has loved. They may come and stand at one's side as several have with me, and show one what they have become. It's all so complicated. But if we are to go further we must recapture the feeling of those lives, and the skills that went with them.

Now I will take a life far back in Britain, when I was at Glastonbury. I wore only a one-piece gown and was nearly always cold. I saw that the only way to warm my body was through prayer – reuniting with the Divine Flame. This gave me the first push towards using the power of thought and visualisation. I became quite proficient, and laughed at the novices.

Easter Sunday, 1985   *Sally*

Oh Mummie, thank you for that letter. I do love to hear a directly voiced thought like this. I know you want to see me. Well that is difficult, but I promise that when you come over I shall be there, just the same Sally that I was on earth. I met Aunt Helen in my old form, but I do not keep it for very long. We, who have been over for some time, gradually lose the need for form. Colour and sound still remain, but you will on occasions find me quite formless. There is no need for you to think of me as that, think of me as the Sally you know. I am just the same underneath, but I've grown a lot wiser (I hope)!

Now to my grandparents. Yes, I saw them when I came over and from time to time, but they have now gone into other spheres, I don't think Grandpa has re-incarnated, I think I should have known, but it may be so. Grandma I think is still in the higher etheric. She was wonderful to me when I came over, and arranged for me to meet and grow among souls of my own vibration.

There is a very deep division on some levels between the generations. I know you all feel it between your generation and mine, but it was was forming between yours and the former one. They were so certain they had all the answers. Now everything we thought we knew has to be reversed, until for a dizzy moment we could not think that we knew anything: that is where learning on our plane begins. We sit very lightly in the thought saddle, reach out and re-adjust at any time, it's a wonderful feeling of expansion, and it still goes on . . . I do not know if there is any end until we have expanded in order to accept the whole of our planet. I am always excited by discovering new things and people on this lovely globe. Entering into it is surprising at every turn. The souls that live inside the Earth are as varied as those outside, But I think they are more advanced. Its difficult to say, because advancement can be on so many levels. Have I made you dizzy with this view of life? Many who come over with set ideas are so hampered by this that they decide to stay and await further enlightenment, and this doesn't really get them anywhere: you must do it yourself. So those who just wait . . . have to re-incarnate, there is no other alternative. Of course some want to go back to finish a work or to be with a dearly loved friend, who they may find is in the act of dying, and the work may either have ceased or gone on beyond their reach. Never go back is my motto. Now I have so many irons in the fire it would be very difficult for me to re-incarnate unless there was an urgent call, this happens when a world war breaks out, and many from here choose to go back. I can't feel that any war would call me! but then I'm just Sally!

Now T.P. is getting very worried that I'm going to use all the power. Good health my darling Mummie, you have been a tower of strength to me on this side, just by knowing, that you knew that I was alive. I want to give back some of that confidence to you and the health to enjoy it.

Sal.

Alexias, how good of Sally to let me in, she does so love writing with you and Cynthia, it gives her quite another element. All these interchanges between people and things bring about chemical reactions in the aura, and you are changed just by a chance blending with another thought force.

I am often in the moon that is really my base now, if one can really have a base; but thought forces draw me away in many directions. for instance Easter is a very exciting New Year's day for us. We all meet often on Earth or on some etheric planet devoted to Christ. These etheric planets are very wonderful, they are the keepers of evolved thought. It took me a long time before I was sufficiently advanced to go there, but when I succeeded it was absolute bliss. Harmony, of a very advanced type, living in close touch with Christ, and hearing His voice and seeing the beautiful etheric body, discarding our own forms completely, but of course I was not sufficiently evolved to stay in that sublime atmosphere for long, so again I was back at square one plus so much to digest, that the world I lived in had to be remade on a higher pattern. These etheric worlds are being used to redeem not only earth, but many other earths that have fallen away; so it is necessary to use the unseen spheres as training grounds.

How you will enjoy all the exquisite channels through which power flows. It's so vast I used to feel worried by the Immensity, but I don't now. We grow naturally equal to the vastness of the universe in which we have been placed.

My love to you my dearest, I am always within call, and eager to do your bidding . . .

W. T. P.

AUNTIE PEG

Nov. 26th 1984   *Sally*
*Auntie Peg is tremendous, she is launching out all over the place, finding out how the trees grow, how the birds awaken the bulbs in the Spring with their song, and how the trees think! She has been living in a tree, a great oak, a real personality who has been teaching her so much Nature lore and fascinating her. Also the link trees have with the sun amazed her, and she says she must train and go off to the sun at the first chance. Of course so far she has not been through the gravitational barrier, but I'm sure she will. I love being with her. At present the earth in all its varying ways, animal and vegetable is holding her here.

Aunt Helen? Yes she is awake, and very glad to have finished her earth life. Dogs and horses clatter round her as personal friends and individuals. It's a most amusing sight. She was met by all her old ones, and every animal she had ever loved streamed up demanding to be remembered. I love being with her, and I am learning more about their ways of thought and feeling. The horses are so intelligent, I can feel now, as she does, that they are not just one move away from us, but that some are definitely on a higher plane. The dogs are often very much the same. They have opened to me a whole series of vibrational planes, and shown me unexplored gifts and abilities. The animal world is here to teach us our lack of power to use the vibrations around us. Dogs and cats can show us how to draw life and healing out of a flower, a tree, or even a nettle! What do you think of that? . . .

Nov 27th Evening   *Sally*
Yes I am here again, this is lovely. Now to try and tell you about my life here. The immensity of it almost frightened me, as each curtain withdrew, showing me the enormous advance into pure spirit. When I say 'Pure Spirit', I mean on the lowest rung of the ladder, but *life* without any physical vibes. When I enter this territory I am formless, dependent only upon Spirit vibes for seeing, hearing and communicating. At first this is a challenge, but very soon it becomes

---

* My sister Beatrix. R. L.

quite natural in the area where the new etheric planets are being created: one can almost smell the concoctions of new life! Scent remains long after all physical life has been withdrawn. I discovered this on my first voyage of discovery outside the Solar System, when I was making for the Milky Way! . . . It was hard work, but not so hard as leaving earth. 'Ce n'est que le premier pas qui côute,' as we used to say, and once outside the power of the moon's rays I was free of our solar system. The sun didn't bother me much although I owe it so much. I thanked the great Sun Spirit as I passed on to others looking very much like him, and our sun bowed and forgave my passing! I must tell you one does experience a darkness on leaving the sun. I felt utterly lost for a short time, until Hugh Dowding's voice rallied me to expect a change. He said, 'Come on, we've only just begun, now we must think ourselves on to the same point in Space-Time.' I replied, 'I'm absolutely "out". I must leave that to you. Tell me what to do.' He said, 'Draw into your mind the vision of a great new planet created entirely of rays. The colours will be staggering almost hypnotising, but don't worry it will pass, and keep your own identity by repeating 'I am Sally, I am learning to use and see what lies beyond the universe.' It was so vast, I couldn't help saying, 'Where does Christ come in? Is He here?' 'Why Yes.' was Hugh's reply, 'Or *we* shouldn't be here. Christ the Logos is Universal. We pinned Him onto a cross and nailed Him into a church. But He doesn't belong there. Don't you feel that you are part of Christ, the part that gives you power to adventure out and out into the Real Eternity' . . . I said, 'Oh Hugh, this is too vast for me, can't you water it down?' We were both laughing by this time and the planet of rays which we had drawn into being was laughing too, while I remained trying to say, 'I am Sally.' to myself and struggling to reconcile all these emotions. Luckily Hugh remains so completely himself that he makes it all seem quite natural.

How deeply we allowed the rays of our own making to flood through our being I cannot say, but eventually I felt stabilised and able to take on these lovely rays, which were of course Christ-given and threaded with all His power. I felt secure, Christ was there, and I was able to see and feel His real strength. This is beyond words, I can only say TRY to understand and exert your image-making of a real and brilliant world from which can be drawn in every kind of help that you need.

I wasn't able to remain indefinitely on this vibe, I soon felt myself

57

slipping back into the old earth vibes, and I was glad to be home again fresh and invigorated by my first experience of the Great Unknown.

Now my darling Mummie I have used all the power, and I must stop with a big kiss, and thank you for coming all this way to talk to me. I will do all I can to make things easier for you.

Blessings upon you my darling . . .

From

Sal

LETTERS FROM EDITH WOOD

Foreword by Margaret Godley

Edith Wood – known to her friends as Edie – died at the age of 56 at Idbury Manor, in the Cotwolds. During her last two years she endured much suffering, but always with supreme courage and faith. She never lost her sense of humour, and her gaiety and thought for others shone like a beacon upon us all.

Our paths crossed in London in 1950, after which we became friends and eventually partners in what turned out to be a momentous and fascinating experiment in the further education of girls. We launched an independent enterprise (named Look and Learn) which offered a year's course of lectures and visits of observation, based on the contemporary scene and on world affairs.

In 1963 we left London and moved to the village of Idbury, where increasing numbers of students enrolled for Look and Learn courses over a period of ten years.

My friend Edie was a rare and gifted personality. Her love for people shone in her face, which radiated light, and her brilliant mind and high intelligence attracted both young and old. She has left a great gap behind her, and memories that can never be forgotten.

Thanks, however, to the initiative and selfless help of our friend Cynthia Sandys, letters from Edie have come through from the 'other side', expressed in her own unmistakeable style, and I can only hope that many of those who read them may feel enlightened and enriched.

In the following scripts the name Pat refers to Patricia, who died over 20 years ago. She was able to get in touch with her mother, Lady Sandys, and since then has been a great help to her, especially when asked to find those who had recently left the earth-plane.

On October 17th, 1976 I visited Cynthia Sandys who asked Pat to find Edie. The first script then came through.

[*Pat*] Ma, I'm so glad to write for Miss Godley – Margaret to me now. But I must go to find this other friend who has come over and is very close to Margaret.

Yes, she is sleeping, this curious half conscious sleep, taking in

59

subconsciously much from her surroundings, and rebuilding confidence into her new ageless diseaseless body. I do not want to disturb this very important phase of life. Tell Margaret she is superbly comfortable and intensely alive and interested in all the new developments around her. When she has absorbed all she needs we will write again. A very interesting woman.

(*Long pause*)

[*Pat*] Ma, I have been watching Edie. She is on the edge of wakefulness; it's not an unconscious sleep. She has been shown and taught the nature of her last life and death and the meaning now to which it has all been put. I will try and ask if she may like to send a message to Margaret. I don't think she will write herself yet. It was such a long illness to get out of her system.

[*Edie*] Yes, I do want to send a message to Margaret. She has been my twin soul for so long and kept me in touch with life. It was necessary both for her and for me to undergo that last test of illness and pain. She suffered as much or even more than I did, and has gained through this joint test.

I want her to know that when I left my body I was instantly free of pain – just like that – and then I was told that I should never suffer pain again and that I was now free of the body physical. You can't imagine my joy at having got through death. It was so simple, so beautiful and so life giving. I became young again immediately. I was slender and agile and gay. I was dancing and throwing myself about as much as I could, but I was out of control of this new featherweight body, I could not believe it.

This Death is a miracle – so swift, so final and it gives one a sense of such security. All the old faith in Goodness returned and I felt myself bathed in the love of God. There is no other way to describe this sense of ultra-well-being, and yet it hardly seemed to be me. I was inhabited by some spirit of power and light unknown to me and yet exactly the vibration that I could hold and harmonise with. I was in an ecstasy of the senses of Love and Light and Radiance. This may sound extravagant to you, but nothing could excel the loveliness, the beauty and the complete belongingness which I was registering. I could go on for ever expatiating on the joy of Death, but I want you to know more. I came in time to a sense of stillness, then complete silence, which was even more fundamentally life-giving. I felt as though all the foundations of my personality

60

were being re-laid. I came to know that I was being taught to be still and to learn within a state of sublime attention. I have been drawing in the knowledge which some day I will pass on to you. Now I must stop. I have used up all the power for the time being. Remember, I am having the time of my life – it's beyond the telling!

Edie

October 18th 1975

[*Pat*] Oh, Ma, it's quite easy to bring Edie to talk to you. She is such a pet and such an extrovert. Here she is:-

[*Edie*] Margaret, this is marvellous. Cynthia, I have been longing to do just this. Oh, I can't tell you how excited I am at every turn of my life. I have just been asked to heal and teach and try to influence children and young people. First I was taken to the place where the children wake up and I was asked to look after some of the toddlers who were calling for Mummy and their pet toy. I was told to look within the child's aura for the shape and colour of the toy and then think it into being in their arms. This works. You can't believe it but it does. I saw elephants and teddy bears and rabbits and I think I did quite well! Then I went to on to older children and teenagers, more my line, and *how* I tried to help them. They were so broken-hearted, as they'd been home and no-one had seen or recognised them. I could have cried for them. But, against all this, the atmosphere is so alive and so happy; the light seems to be threaded with laughter if that makes sense, and we cannot, literally cannot, be unhappy for long within the range of these wonderful rays. No, I won't write much tonight, I'm only getting my thoughts together; tomorrow I shall have much more to say.

All my love and a much richer love than I ever had to give on earth; here it seems to come through me straight from the Throne of God.

Edie

October 19th 1975

Cynthia, how lovely that you should both sit and think of me in this way. I have not yet understood how this can be done, but your delightful Patricia has shown me that you and she can do it quite easily. Well, I have been spending the most wonderful time living in a lovely garden with a lake and hills all round, and meeting such clever and intellectual people, who were ready and willing to answer

61

my questions and explain this new way of living, where there is no disease and no want of any kind. One only has to think one's wish and the condition appears before one. I am in a crowd of wonderful people of all races who are comparing, discussing and answering my questions. I will not say more tonight, but tomorrow. My love to you both.

Edie

December 3rd 1975

I began to take in Light. This is quite a new sensation. It's almost like eating and drinking. It becomes part of our body and with it we become lighter in weight and are surrounded by radiance. I found that many of the others had done this during life and were easily airborne on arrival, which I was not. Now I am trying to learn how to extend my *light* body so that it will lift me into the upper ether. It's a most exciting experiment and there are always people ready to help. I found when I could leave the Earth that on looking back it was covered by a grey mass of tiny lines. I asked what it was, and was told that they were earthbound thoughts; the earth people are always thinking down and never up. As I got lighter I found that the Light became intense, so intense that I had to return to my own vibration. 'That is what you have to get used to,' they told me. We must use the Armour of Light to protect ourselves against this greater Light.

All my love,
Edie

May 4th 1976

Yes, Cynthia, I am growing up in this wonderful world with all the understanding I had acquired in ordinary life. This means so much. I came into the earth life without any conscious knowledge or understanding and now I can peep into a new set of conditions with all the clear reasoning power that was given in life to my Scottish mind. Margaret will laugh at that remark! I was always looking for the reason below everything and discarding it utterly if I didn't find a good enough reason. Here it is all as clear as crystal, and I sometimes wonder why I hadn't seen it all before. Then I stand back and laugh at myself for having been so critical. I see now the reasons behind all the changes in my life, and how I came to meet Margaret and decide to work with her. It is now obvious that she and I had worked and played and planned together during several lives. We had both been teachers before but in different lands. I was in Rome and she was in Florence, and then she found me in Rome and we both belonged to a great teaching order of Nuns. This was, I should think, the sequel to the hundreds of lives before that when we had both been soldiers and fought together through several of those frightful wars where religion, so called, played a part. I fell in one of these many fights, and Margaret looked after me with wonderful care. Then we were apart for some time, but met again later. I have all this from the Akashic records. I think I can read them. I am eager for Margaret to share my life in this way if that is possible. I have sought to look back and back and back to our beginnings. I have been in touch with alchemists and prophets and soothsayers and all kinds of people who had the Sight right back in Time, until the moment before Man's soul had completely lost intimate touch with Divinity. The early men of pre-history were like children living without an all-pervading soul, and that was why they did such ghastly things. But as they grew the soul became closer to man and further from the Divine Source. This was the intention, for man was to learn to grow his own Divinity through an inherent memory of God, and gradually to return consciously to this state. Now we see that you in the body are waking up to this ideal, and when I speak of these old lives they all hold a key to our present power to grow and grow. The end of this must be of such a 'Dimension of Freedom' that your mind boggles at the very thought, and I am content to move slowly step by step taking it all in and acknowledging the greatness and the beauty and the love which carries the whole universe, with all the attendant etheric planes, to a perfection beyond all understanding. Now I must stop and say thank you for taking time to work with me again. My dearest love to Margaret and a great hope that she may perhaps hear or even see me one day.

Edie.

June 17th 1976
Yes, this is my birthday and you have been eating strawberries and now you two, Cynthia and Margaret, are thinking of me and wondering if I have strawberries over here! Well, yes, I do – we can all think and visualise our food and when I thought strawberries I saw them big and round and very sweet; they are nectar to me, but I don't think our sense of taste goes on forever – it all seems rather

63

superfluous, but for today great fun. What am I doing? Well, it's hardly a routine. I am sampling life between the planes. I shall settle soon but not immediately. They urge us to spend as long as we like trying to sample other lives. I haven't left the earth completely yet. I feel that there is something to be done here, but the upper ether is entrancing. I am again urged not to spend too much time trying out my wings so to speak, but to search out all my old friends and pupils and try to help them *now* when I still have so many physical vibrations. This is important, so I tried to get in touch with everyone I taught at Idbury, and that took some doing. Most of them were completely happy in their marriages, family, work, with children and home. Of course, I often go into the kitchen and suggest ideas, especially to our old students, but it's very hard to get ideas through unless people have questing auras. This means that the aura goes out with a searching ray that I can pick up as I do sometimes, and then we cook together which, of course, means that she is delighted with a result that she could never quite accomplished alone. All the young and old whom we knew and loved are debts from other lives. We have to pay off anything that they feel they have lost on our account. I am not very good at doing this because they need something which I personally am unable to give, and must go outside myself to find and bring into their auras.

I did this lately with a girl who was unhappily married. I did not know what to do, so I went and sat at the feet of Wisdom and was told to awaken in her a sense of patience so that she in her turn might pay back a debt which she had incurred during another life; she must now wipe it out through patience and love. The man seemed very surly to me, but in another life she had borne him as a child who was unwanted, and she had turned him out altogether. Now she has to bear with him until her debt is paid and she has acquired a love for him. Here I sense in love a mood, an energy, a vital principle in life; I can handle it and fold it into her aura . . . but it is hard to make it stick. Many great souls come and help us. I have only to ask for help and they come. Did you ask had I met your Mother, Margaret? Yes, of course I have and she's one of the people who teach one how to handle the love element.

We laugh at ourselves in all these forms until we are worn out or depleted, without sense, and then in the wink of an eyelid we are away up in the air or down in the sea, swinging over the ocean bed, lighted by a thousand beams unseen by human eye in a fairyland of colour. Oh, my dear Cynthia, I could go on for ever about the beauty and interest of this life and how it all fits in, but I have taken enough of your power.

Give my love to Margaret and tell her that some part of me is always with her and can be recalled in a moment to help. I know you are thinking it's time I stopped all this chatter.

Goodnight, I am free, alive and riotously well.

Edie.

July 30th 1976

Life over here is so exciting. To begin with I had to learn to walk again, then I was shown the lakes and invited to bathe and told I should feel so much stronger if I could face up to the water, which would be warm and pleasant. So I went through all the silly desire to undress, and when told to walk in just as I was I felt so stupid; but the miracle happened. I was in the water and instantly quite free of all clothing. It was LOVELY! I was met by the water. It was life-giving and even scented with a thousand flowers. I don't know how long I stayed in the water, but when I came ashore I was no longer embarassed at being without clothes. My body was young and slender and I felt how good it was to have such a body and I became quite proud of it! Could it be true after all these years of trailing a heavy body? It just couldn't be true, but they all laughed and hurried me on to dive into yet another lake. This was a sparkling pool of the most vivid glorious blue sapphire water. I lay in and on the water . . . listening . . . the water was speaking sometimes in verse, sometimes in prose, sometimes in music. I lay in ecstasy listening and trying to take it all in, but of course I couldn't, and very soon I became so tired they said, 'Come and rest. You've done more than enough.' So I came out and lay in the air. Yes, not ON anything. It was delightful and I was so light, in fact, weightless and this was another miracle. We go through one after another . . . sound, colour and form, all changing in their various ways.

When I woke up after a gorgeous sleep I found I was alone with a beautiful woman unknown to me. She took my hand and said, 'You do not remember me but we have been close sisters in another life, in fact lives, and now we are together again.

I have been your guardian in your last life, that is one who assists the Guardian Angel and who is closer to your vibration.'

I did not recognise her at all and could not remember anything.

She sat beside me and took my hands and suddenly, click . . . it happened just as if you had switched on the T.V. I was standing with her in a ship. We were prisoners, taken, I think, from Scotland by the Vikings and horribly frightened. She said, 'Don't let fear worry you. I had to use a violent emotion to draw your memory out of its dormant condition. Now we can go further.' I was on a farm. We were ploughing and it was very sterile soil and so little of it. I think it was Norway. I loved the rough work in spite of having to be used in this way. There were no horses or oxen in the picture, but I had a feeling of a gay and convivial people. They were awaiting a King's return. I think it was Scotland and I had a feeling of Edinburgh and Holyrood. I stood very still and tried to see and feel and then I saw her – Mary, Queen of Scots, lovely and sad and so alluring . . . I fell immediately under her spell. That faded, too, but I will try and tell you more tomorrow. The power has gone. My dearest Cynthia, all my love to you both.

Edie

August 17th 1976
I went one day and sat on the cliff overlooking the sea. 'Come on,' said the others, 'Let's go and slip down the face of the cliff.' I was suddenly terrified, and all the old, heavy ME took charge. I said, 'I can't,' but they took my hand and made me jump into the air, and then, of course, instead of falling I was looking intently into the sea birds' nests on the very edge of the cliff, and soon we slipped slowly into the green water below. "Now we'll go on to the caves," they said, and I was again frightened. I love the sea, but I didn't want to go under the sea; again I was reminded that my breathing was not of the earth now and that I should feel no stifling sense of drowning, only a fuller freer sense of reality. So, I took a deep breath and went down with them, and I was so excited by all that I saw I quite forgot that I was breathing quite naturally very far down indeed. It all seemed to be lighted by an unearthly ray, and at last I realised that the light, at least much of it, was coming from ourselves. I was throwing out a ray of light as I turned and twisted, and so did the comprehensive torch which had become my body. Into this light came all manner of creatures . . . fish of some sort, but mainly tiny etheric beings of the sea, endless in variety and number, glistening in all kinds of colours and giving out rays too. I was utterly enchanted by this Fairyland and said so to my companions, whom I

had clean forgotten . . . and suddenly I realised that they were no longer with me! Terror seized me again. How could I struggle back alone?

I tried to rise in the water, but I was in a cavern, and only hit my head against solid rock! . . . Then suddenly the rock gave way and I was struggling through a grey mist with the water gushing all round. I could move and think more clearly and now I began to wish most urgently that I could reach the surface and sunlight which I understood. Just then the rock gave way to water. A big fish-like creature brushed past me and I found myself calling upon him or her to help me to regain the surface. He turned his head, a great cod-like head, and snuffled me as though he'd heard and understood, and with a wave of his tail I found I was being gently propelled to the surface and the sunlight. I turned to thank my rescuer, but all I heard was a sigh and a rush of water as he turned to resume his original path below.

Oh, how glad I was to be at home in the sunlight, and there was the cliff and the sea birds' nests, and I called in thankfulness upon all who had drawn me back to the land of sunlight and to things I knew and loved. As I lay on the surface just thanking and feeling relaxed and at peace my Guides returned to me, and I welcomed them with a slight coolness for having deserted me in the hour of my greatest need. All they said was, 'It was a test for you, now you know you can deal with all life once you CALL for help; you have done well.'

I was so grateful and glad to know, but I said, 'You might have warned me.'

'We have often told you these things but you took no notice when we were there, so we just had to leave you to it. Be prepared for the next. It will come sooner or later in space or earth or under earth. You must learn to draw from outside yourself, and inside yourself; you are like lightning coming from above and being met from below.'

Edie

August 18th 1976

Now, I first learnt that I was completely weightless . . . no cliffs or chasms alarm me any more; I am self-sufficient in my power to pass through matter as I did through the rock of the cavern. I also learnt that I must NOT panic; that was very distressing and brought me into a lower vibration which made it impossible for me to concentrate and visualise my next move. You have no idea how important this is. Then I learnt that I could talk to the fishes and the dear old cod who helped me to regain the surface. I can get my thoughts into their minds, but they must be simple and direct. After my Guides had rejoined me we went back slowly up the cliff, and on the way I tried speaking to the gulls who were nesting in the rock, but they were far too busy with family life to listen; so I paused directly in front of a lovely bird, not a gull, I think some other kind, I haven't got the name; he or she was sitting comfortably on the nest, and I asked her if she had laid all her eggs. The reply was, 'Yes, but I may lose some and have to re-lay; there are so many dangers here. Other gulls steal. Oh, how they steal . .' and she went into a long harangue which I couldn't follow about the crimes committed by her neighbours, so I sympathised and moved on to a nest of fledgings. Here they were far too busy and agitated to talk to me as the first flight was in progress, and this meant that the little birds were about to go through my experience of stepping into the air and trying their wings for the first time, with the deadly peril of the sea below and any predators who might catch them on the way. My Guides said at once, 'Come and help, you will learn more about flying.' I was close to the first little bird, who flapped in panic on leaving the nest and then got her balance in the air and made it quite easily. I waited for the second and that went well, but the third was smaller and not so strong, and on the way I saw a kite swerving towards him. I rushed to intercept and beat him off, but with no effect, until my Guides cried, 'Call him, call him and make him frightened. He can hear your voice but can only see you dimly.' So I called and yelled and frightened him. He thought a man was near and flew off while my little bird scurried away into a crevice half way down the cliff. I was fascinated. Could I help again? 'Yes,' they said, 'we often come and do this as it's very vital and helps so many of the nestlings to breed and escape.'

After staying for some time going up and down the cliff in this way I found that my flying was immensely more easy to manage. I could control and even do a few acrobatics and this gave me confidence, so I began asking my Guides, 'What next?'

'Well, you must learn now to go further into the world of nature; they need your help at every turn, the trees, the crops and the flowers.' I was interested and asked again, 'How?'

'Well, you have the vital spark of LIFE, and that you can spread among all living things. Go out and experiment with them.'

I'd rather work with animals and I asked if I could help with farm animals – calves and lambs on the cliffs or in the market.

They said, 'Try everything in the wild first. Don't go into the market until you are fully trained or your emotional pity will swamp your power to save.'

So, there I am now with a whole new world to conquer. I am fascinated and I think I shall go back to the sea to help the sea creatures first as a thank offering for the way I was saved and protected on my first expedition.

All my Love,
Edie

September 21st 1976

Yes, I am here. I've come from Space! Think of that, Margaret! Space! I am getting off the ground and doing a lot more flying. It's wonderful; you can't imagine this bliss and the freedom as I go off and up and up until, I suppose, I am as high as Everest or higher, then suddenly I feel frightened and say to myself, 'Now I must keep calm and float down as I've been taught and soon they will come and call me and I'll go off to the moon.' But not yet. They are very strong about training and, of course, I had to start from scratch and this weightlessness is so exciting sometimes I feel I'm not there at all, or anywhere, and then what am I? I was in a real worry one day, and a voice said to me, 'You are neither more nor less than your thoughts – fabric you are living out – meditate, draw in and give out – that is you.'

I said, 'Oh, yes, but can't I be more than that?'

I want to tell you about the air crash and the sea crash that have just happened in your atmosphere. Pat called me to come and see and help those just coming over. She said I was so full of physical vibrations that I could get quite close to the victims of this disaster. I went with her into lovely country, and there in the air, on the ground and among the rocks and trees everywhere we found people trying to understand what had happened. They were in a dazed condition. Pat and *Flo took them far away from all signs of the crash and made them sit down and rest. They were told this accident had happened, but that they were only suffering from shock and must rest and eat and drink something.

* Flo refers to Florence Nightingale, first cousin to Patricia's grandmother.

'Now what would you like?' said Pat in a most practical voice. 'A glass of sherry or a cup of tea?'

'Oh, tea,' said most of them, 'tea and toast.'

'So it shall be,' said Pat with a lovely smile, and before you could count ten there were steaming hot cups of tea and buttered toast smelling delicious. We all handed it round and the moment they had swallowed some tea and eaten a mouthful they instantly became natural, calm, understanding people.

'Tell us how we get home from here,' was the first question.

'That will be arranged,' they were told, but some were anxious about friends and relations they had been with and had not yet been found. So we all went out as search parties and of course those who came with us saw the frightful chaos of the place and realised that many people had been killed. But they kept on saying, 'How fortunate for us that we escaped without a scratch.'

Gradually we gathered them all in and they were, of course, convinced that they were alive and well and wanted their families to know as soon as possible. So an etheric office was constructed and they were given the chance to write the names and addresses of those whom they wanted to cable. Then they were suddenly so very, very weary and they all strayed back and lay down to sleep until, as we told them, the plane would come and take them home.

I'm sorry to have used all the power to tell of this but it was so exciting for me to see the other side of the tragedy I couldn't bear to waste a moment. I'll tell you more tomorrow.

My dearest love,
Edie

September 22nd 1976

I want to tell you about the ship that sank. I wasn't there but I've been there since it happened. I don't know how quickly those men trapped in the ship were able to leave their bodies, but I gather it was fairly rapid and quite unexpected. Having got free, of course, they were able to lift themselves on to the surface and were soon helping to raise the submerged ship. It was the most extraordinary scene. When Pat took me there I found a number of ships round the sunken one, with men climbing about in and out of the water. At first I couldn't distinguish those in the body from those out of the body. To me they looked the same until Pat explained that those in our sort of bodies were plunging down without diving suits and

70

coming up shouting to the rest, giving directions which no-one seemed to understand, going up to their old mates and bellowing in their ears, but there was no response. I saw a look of utter amazement in the face of one obviously able seaman when no orders he'd given were carried out.

'What can we do?' I asked Pat.

'Call a halt and ask them all to come aft for a drink.'

We did so – they were thirsty – but couldn't see her.

Next time I looked at Pat she'd taken on the look and uniform of a seaman. 'I'm making them see me now,' she said. 'If we can get them to relax and drink hot coffee we'll get them to sleep, and then they can be taken away from all this, and cease to feel frustrated.'

Pat looked very well and commanding as she issued her orders for a break and hot drinks to be provided, as before, out of the ether. The steaming hot coffee had the same instant effect of releasing them and they relaxed and were soon lying fast asleep. Then came the next stage. Others, I suppose of the Angels, came and carried the sleeping forms away, wrapt in a cloud of Light. I was so astonished that I just stood and waited. Pat said they were using my physical vibrations all the time, and this gave me great pleasure. We can be useful coming over and we learn to do more and more. I asked what was going to happen when these people from both crashes woke up. 'They don't all wake at once. Some sleep for quite a long time and others only a very short time, but we are able to get some of their relations who are already here to meet them.'

All love,
Edie

November 17th 1976

Cynthia, I am glad to be with you both again.

Many of my friends came over with entities who were doing them no good; one could see this and one often said, 'Do stop smoking or drinking or drugs' and they looked so hopeless one dropped the subject. But now I know it was not they who were speaking but the entities – the 'familiars' who had grown into their auras. This is a terrible dilemma, and how to clear these auras of them has been one of my tasks. It is a definite rooted growth on the aura, which assails the mind and often causes physical illness and great instability. How many things there are in the atmosphere! I have been back to Egypt to re-live one of my lives there and learn, or re-learn some of the old wisdom of the Sphinx and the Pyramids. You would do well to use the form of a Pyramid. It has a focusing form of great power. When I asked why there were no Pyramids in other parts of the world I was told that the Pyramid had been mis-used and was too potent to be used selfishly; so be careful. When I first came here I lived from hour to hour seeing and sensing and learning how to assimilate and give out. It's a long, slow way of recovery. But we do it in glorious surroundings and the spirit body reacts so quickly to the extraordinary atmosphere which carried such buoyancy. There is no weight or gravitation to pull one down, and in the very mode of live movement thought is so rapid. We don't have meals or sleep, so night and day are not here, but a fine variety of life, form and occupation come to us.

All these bodies are very perplexing. I knew I had a spirit body and possibly an astral, but I had no idea about the higher body, the Greater Self or the Group Soul. Am I going too quickly now? I've got the knack again. I think I should tell you more about them tomorrow, but I want to give you a picture of life. No routine of living – no day or night – but constant changes in the flow of space and time. I found a dear girl with me who was just as confused, and we tried to regulate the space time – with no success until she said, 'There must be others who understand. Let's sit still and call for help,' and in due course a very nice man came to our aid. He said he'd been an astronomer and become used to thinking in these terms. I said, 'What was your name in your last life?' 'Oh, Jeans,' was the simple answer. So then I knew that I was in safe hands. Just think of calling upon Professor Jeans to disentangle our first complexities!

March 21st 1977
I was staggered by the thought of how little we knew of earth – only living on the surface and such a short way up into the clouds; I was fascinated by earth and the great earth spirits. I had no idea that Pan really existed outside fairyland and was staggered and overcome when I met this great Spirit; and rather frightened. He spoke to me and said, 'I am only Pan, the preserver of all life, don't be frightened of me. It's only the Church that gave me this name and made the word "panic" out of it. All life on this planet responds to me and I work under the Christ Leadership. If you want to enter the earth take my vibration and slip inside.' So down I went like Alice

72

in Wonderland, but it was not dark or gloomy, and everything seemed to be surrounded by light.

I looked around for Pan to be my guide, but saw no-one. I was rather lost and lonely and not a little frightened, and then I heard a laugh quite close. I called to the owner to come and help me, as I was lost. 'Not lost, no-one here is lost,' was the reply, 'But I will show you fairyland if that is what you are seeking. Here we grow all the soils and seeds and minerals for the use of Man, but they do not understand and think it is all their doing. Here we mix and grow and give life, otherwise there would be no life in the little brown seeds which you grow. Everything on the surface starts here, so we are very busy.' I looked and lingered and asked questions about food and vegetables. 'Oh, they grow here too but Man puts such awful things on them to make them grow bigger that they are sometimes very bad for the human body.' I went further into the area of the metals and this was exciting because many of them do not consist only of earth materials and vibrations, but are alloyed by the stars direct. Rays come from various Stars far outside our vision, with the most glorious vibrations, and they produce what we call precious stones – diamonds and rubies. These, if used in conjunction with those vibrations could and should be of immense power in healing – in creating harmony and promoting growth. I said, 'Don't tell me too much at once. How can I use a diamond, for instance?'

'Look at it, see all the colours radiating from it. Absorb them into your own aura and send them out to anyone in need of strength or harmony. Man never does this, so all these lovely power centres remain unused.'

I said, 'Thank you, I have learned all, or more, than I can understand. May I go now to my garden of recuperation and think all these things over.'

All my love,
Edie

April 12 1977
You can't think what a stabilising effect you both have. *You* live in a tiny cell with walls too well defined, while I have no limits to my power if I am concentrated. It's all too big and I sometimes lose confidence in myself. I know this will make you laugh! I have always thought I knew best, but now I am comforted by those who are even less able to cope than I am. I was shown and taken about as I told

you, then I was left alone to make my new life – very hard if you have no direct leadership. I wanted a set of rules and a map to explain where to go and what to see, but they said, 'Go and find out.' I made a few excursions on my own, learning to fly higher and land and steer and get to places I wanted to see again, but I lacked a guide and a companion. At last I said, 'Do give me someone who knows,' and at once a charming woman was at my side. 'Why didn't you invite me before?' was her first remark after I'd given her a great welcome.

'Oh,' I replied weakly, 'didn't I?'

'No, you may have wanted to, but you must ask for friends and relations; they don't come automatically; it's a "Do it Yourself" world here.'

I felt rather shamed, and so we sat down and talked and she explained a lot and then suggested I should learn to help people. 'What sort of people?' I asked.

'That is for you to choose – clever or stupid, young or old; those who have suffered illness or infirmity for years need a lot of help to learn that they are no longer ill.'

I love children and young people, but I had never tried to awaken minds towards health, so I said, "Take me to the old sufferers.' In no time I was in a sort of hospital ward, but there were trees and grass and flowers and the walls seemed only shadowy. I was taken to an old woman sitting humped up in a chair quite close to the wall. I went up to her and asked if she was feeling well.

'No, I'm not, and this is a horrid draughty place; don't you see that they've never finished building the walls?' I looked, but could feel no draught, only a lovely warm sunshine. I said, 'Won't the sun do you more good?'

'No, it's my arthritis – I can't walk and the cold makes it so much worse.'

'Shall I push you into the garden to a sheltered spot?' I suggested.

'I don't think you can find one, but try. I'm sick and tired of this ward with no nurses.'

'Have you asked for one?' I ventured, having just learned the answer to that one.

'Well no, but they ought to be here.'

'I think they come when your thought calls them,' I answered.

She looked at me as though I'd gone mad and then said:

'It's all very strange here. I sometimes think it's all a dream and I

74

shall wake up at home cold and aching. It's always worse on waking.'

'But are you in pain now?' I went on.

'N-No, I suppose I'm not.'

'Not at all?'

'No, I really feel quite well here if it wasn't all so strange. I haven't seen a doctor,' she went on grumbling.

'Well, never mind, if you are out of pain let's go into the garden.'

We did. I thought her chair looked awfully heavy, but it was a featherweight and we slid over the grass and up the hills to a lake beyond.

'Oh, how lovely!' she burst out suddenly. 'I do like this. I wonder where it is.'

'The outer courts of Heaven,' I heard myself saying and she looked at me in astonishment.

'Then I'm dead,' she screamed, 'At last. I never thought I'd die – how wonderful – no pain – no weight and I can stand up and feel like a child.'

Her look of utter joy was such a change from the frowning woman of a short time before. I could hardly believe my eyes. But things had happened to me at the same time. I'd become less fixed, more mobile and with a happy flow of returning confidence. One simply must have confidence.

All my love,
Edie

April 13th 1977

My dear Margaret, you've no idea what a boost you gave me yesterday. It was lovely to be with you both in the library and to hear and see all the things I had known there before. I want to express the enormous need we have for the contact of all those we love on earth. It's so real and so strengthening. It's like champagne – seeing and hearing you. I can see you dimly almost any time but not clearly unless you are concentrating on me. What I call glancing thoughts are not enough. I think the real need we have is for a home. All this is so big that it's too big for me. I haven't grown up to it yet and the only way I rise today is by your help and the help of those few others who know about these things. Physical vibrations are vital to us now and then. We see and hear and are shown, and if we want to create a tiny cottage to live in, well, that's all right, but in the end it limits you, as Cynthia explained. So I was warned against that and I am trying to forge ahead on my own. It's a great challenge, but, of course, we are helped all the time when we ask. I'm not very good at asking, but I often go back to the hospitals to help those who know even less than I do, like the case I told you about yesterday. I have been to the children's side, and that is delightful and everything is done to make them feel at home – their bed and toys and even the house and garden are all duplicated, and the parents are with them during sleep which entirely satisfies most of them. They grow into seasoned etherics in no time.

What I am doing now is to collect the spring in the soul, which petered out during my last illness; I need to WANT to go on. I don't really. I'd like to stay in a cottage and think, and shall probably do just that because I haven't assimilated anything like all I've been shown. So I must confess you have helped me through a bad attack of mental indigestion.

Always yours,
Edie

May 15th 1977

My dear Margaret, this is wonderful and just what we both need – to talk and exchange news. I am now an almost established etheric. I like that term, don't you? It's as though I had passed my exam or done it more or less completely. So I can now do a lot more things. I can get out of my etheric body and be bodiless. Yes, that is quite a thing! One has to be able to do this before one can start on space travel. I am learning so many new crafts. Whereas on earth I always liked cookery and good food, here we get the corresponding art of mixing and refining rays and pouring them into people or things or atmospheres, or even ships and cars. I took quite a lot of my rays and poured them into Cynthia's car for a safe and easy journey and when you left the car and went to Iona. I tried, oh, so hard to help you to carry your cases, but there I failed. It was too physical for me. Iona I found most exciting. I loved being there with you and I couldn't have got there without your help; you can only re-visit places you know and can visualise, unless you can cling on to someone else, like children watching a non-U-film. Well, I came. The whole island is ringed with fire. I could see it from afar and the old Saint comes and goes in the most casual way. Oh, yes, I've met St. Columba and St. Oram and a lot of others. That funny old man

76

whom you said you rather disliked was one of St. Columba's servants who, as he told me in a whisper, was always in revolt and starting a new idea. 'Useful and often disruptive, but I still love him,' was his parting remark.

St. Columba was all sweetness and acquiescence – he said certain things must be endured, others can be averted, and you can only learn through prayer and meditation which is which. I sat at his feet on the hillside overlooking the sea on the atlantic side and listened and listened; he called the birds and the beasts, the rabbits and stoats and weasels and rats; they all came to listen. 'If you don't like my company,' he said one day on seeing some of us new etherics looking oddly at the rats, 'if you don't like my company don't stay, but if you want to stay you must first give out love to all present.' Very salutary and so good for us! I was near some tough looking rats so I threw out a ray and cuddled them to me with great ease and all the while Columba was speaking. I could sometimes understand, and sometimes not understand one word. I think it was in Gaelic but I should have learnt enough of the thought patterns to follow him, but as it was I only followed a few.

Sometimes I wandered on over the island scenting the flow of this wonderful early Christian Druidic teaching.

St. Oram, an ex-Druid, taught Columba the Devic side and gave him the entrée to all the Nature Spirits. It was the most wonderful marriage between the Christ and the Devic Kingdoms which had before been separate. I came in the end to the Abbey and waited for a ritual of the Saints. It was quite beyond description, in fact I think I should like to gather more strength for this. May we pause and then perhaps write again.

May 16th 1977
Cynthia, Yes, I would like to finish my letter about the Abbey and what it is doing on the etheric plane. First of all the colour, the light and the music. At first I found it too much of everything – far too much light and colour such as I had never seen; then the music absolutely drowned me. It was so penetrating, not because it was loud and discordant, but because it seemed to enter into me and resound and vibrate inside me. I couldn't take it at first and just came out and waited about on the hillside. Then, as the booming of the organ became more acceptable, I crept closer and something was urging me to go again inside and I did, closing my eyes and

trying to cover my ears, but we hear all over us with these bodies, to a certain extent. We see, too, so I was seeing through my toes and hands, through my wrists and knees. It's the queerest feeling to have a multiple-sighted, hearing, feeling body. Not altogether a good thing. But there was the challenge. Should I, could I go in and take part in this amazing ritual, and what was it all about? It was a healing service, I was told. 'But what do you need to heal on this side,' I asked. 'Well, come and see,' was the answer.

All this time and for long before I had a feeling that I possessed a sort of shadow following me, and as I entered I found many others with far greater shadows who were also moving up towards the altar. They looked like duplicates walking in perfect precision. I hadn't particularly noticed mine, but others had and I was pushed forward among the crowd. In front of the altar there was an immense flow of light as each couple, that is, the person and the duplicate, reached the light and became separate, one going one way and one the other. I did not know at all what this meant, but I carried on with the crowd and I heard someone say, 'You have to drop your sick body.' But I had no sick body, it was all behind me on earth.

'No, that is just what you all thought,' was the reply. 'If you have been ill for some time you have produced a sick body which grows an entity within itself and lives on you as a parasite.'

This was news to me because I had never allowed my illness to become Me, at least I thought not, so I took a good look at my shadow and sure enough as I reached the altar there was a searing ray thrust between me and my shadow and a sense of loss, almost sadness of parting overtook me as my shadow went one way and I was channelled to the other. It was exhausting and depleting and I wondered how much of Me had gone with my shadow. I asked for help and advice and was told that all illnesses produce this other you (unless you pass out suddenly) and then it remains a part of you which still has life and needs to be given the chance to re-educate itself away from negative illness; or in the case of the very persistent cases it has to be cleansed. Mine, they said, was of quite a gentle nature and would probably be re-absorbed into the grass of Iona.

What a story, isn't it? I was loth to leave my shadow and I felt I could help it to become a flower or an animal, but I was told that that was not to be my line of action. I must not try to get in touch again; we were separated for ever. I looked round at the rest of the 'bereaved' for that is what they looked like. Many of them had become attached to, and reliant on, this other self and were now on their own for the first time for years.

I began to feel better, freer and lighter, more able to move swiftly, and so I began my entirely free life from all physical attachments – these others, sometimes known as 'familiars' were released from us, so a great revision of life had to take place. The Abbey is especially suited for this work, and on one plane it is going on there all the time.

August 19th 1977
Cynthia, I am glad to write. It's such a good way of getting things straight in my own mind as well as in yours and Margaret's. We have so many new things thrust at us that we get rather dishevelled in thought, and I often need to write things down. I do, but writing in the etheric doesn't last, as it fades so quickly, while this is here for ever, and what's more, you can read it whether you close the book or keep it open. That's another lovely thing here. At first I longed to read more of our old Classics. Then, of course, I couldn't move them unless they were given me in small doses, or the books were left open. Now I can read a book by laying my hand on it and telling my mind about it. You've no idea what fun that is. I've done such a lot of reading – first your sort (I mean earth books) and now I can read the atmosphere where all the records of life on all planes are stored.

Now about healing. So many here have never thought of it. I feel so strongly that we are meant to take our mind and energy into the next body at the end of life, and so make it possible to leave it quietly and easily. As one saintly person said to me, 'I just offered my life back to Christ and he took it.' There are people in all kinds of different states of being, some hardly physical at all, who have so much more of the spirit that I can't see how they can go on living.

I met a saintly old priest the other day. He was preparing for another life when I heard him say, 'No, I'll do the new method and slip in and out of a body.'

There are several types of thought-life, and I often move from one to another. I have been more about in the world of Thought; it's another layer of being. One can move from a layer of colour and music to a layer of pure thinking. This is when new worlds are forming in the land of the Supreme Being, but they are too difficult for me to express at this stage.

I don't know how to give you any conception of our life here. There are no divisions of night and day, meals, rest or relaxation. But we are constantly moving from one to the other. I still sleep, but not very often, and then I have breakfast – not because I need it, but because I have the habit when beginning the day. I hope to reach a state when this is not necessary. I eat mainly fruit, – etheric, of course, so clean and life-giving. After it I can run many hundreds of feet, and enjoy all the sensations of flying, but I have much yet to learn before I can enter the stratosphere.

I see it is difficult for you to catch my thoughts. I feel I am putting them into you from all angles, and often seem to miss you altogether. It's because I am not yet completely under control. This is such a world of currents, and I am flung gently this way and that. But I must tell you the earth currents have changed since your Jubilee. We have all been in greater or lesser touch with the Queen. You know what a very great person she is. I wish you could see the magnificent bodyguard she has had from this side – you need not have feared for her safety in Ireland.

All my love,
Edie

August 21st 1977
Now let me think clearly; I have limbs as before and I have senses. I can see now and then with my toes. I can also hear through my hands and, oddest of all, I can understand with my solar plexus. Think of literally thinking with your tummy! I can even talk to my different parts and explain and ask advice. How I wish I'd known of this on earth. I could have done much more thinking and healing during sleep. I have now found that this new unconscious sleep is the most fascinating rhythm of consciousness. One can get outside the body, and yet with sight and hearing we can move, perceive, and know at each step the underlying influences at work on lives at their different levels. If I am with Margaret at her cottage I can see and feel her exact condition of mind and body and at the same time I can see others who are moving about there; some have lived there before, others need to know her and receive power from her and yet others bring their rare gifts of spiritual sight. It's a most tantalising gift, because I haven't yet gathered the concentration of mind to absorb all the

different sides, and I want very much to ask questions, but that can't be done in sleep, and when I am back in my fully conscious body I have so often forgotten the very question that I wanted to ask. I find that I am moving more easily and can get off the ground and reach the clouds. This seemed to me to be a little risky, but they said, 'Go on, you can't fall now! If you get into orbit we'll come and help.' Nothing is still for long and I find that worrying – trees and flowers particularly – the former expand and grow, produce etheric tissues and then further tissues until I've lost sight of the nice comfortable tree which I knew and loved. Flowers are never still for an instant; they radiate immense volumes of colour and sound, and the nature spirits who lead them would delight you with their charm and agility. Food – No, I don't eat much now, but I do have a snack with the new arrivals who still need food to consolidate their thinking. I'm growing on this thought force, and this seems to me so important for you and for all of us and will make communication much easier.

August 23rd 1977
I am so glad we can write again. I am full of things I want to say and explain but I feel terribly inadequate to express them. First of all I want to tell you about teaching over here. There are a few rare leaders who come to give us the sound of thought, not in words, but in the pattern of thought, and we have to read them as best we can. There are others who speak in a multi-volume manner and give to each one the thing they need to know, while no sound reaches the other students regarding the next door neighbours. It's magical and works like the language machine they use on earth, but here there are no language patterns because it is mainly thought and very rapid thought. I found that confusing at first; these etherics take in and understand instantly, and there is no pause. I have learnt something of this word pattern language that does away with foreign tongues, but I am still very much a learner at taking in this direct individual ray of teaching. It's all done out of doors in the most lovely country often beside a river. The water adds enormously to the volume and strength of the message.

I have met several of my old friends from other lives especially in Greece, Rome and Egypt. What a lot of lives we have all lived! I feel quite shattered by the number and often get them mixed up. I have been a man several times and a sailor. I loved the rough-and-tumble

81

life and never quite ceased to long for it. I was, I think, a Venetian; anyway, it was in the Mediteranean. I see one or two scenes quite clearly. I am often fighting and enjoying it enormously. Can you believe it? In Egypt I remember the Nile and the great oars we used, and how grand and great the big ceremonies were. I saw, or think I saw and heard, some of the pyramids being brought into being. There was a great excitement and I could only hold the picture for a moment. Great columns of priests in wonderful gold robes, catching the light and the sound of the sun's rays. I heard the tremendous buzzing as the sun rose, we gathered and prostrated ourselves, and then the air was filled with light and sound. It was so thick with vibrations that I could not see very much until the chanting began, and then I saw huge rocks move of their own volition towards the place selected and they told me a great physical force was being erected. I watched, but saw very little, and when the next scene came within my vision there stood a pyramid, not one of the big ones, but a holy shape and through that the mystical power of Egypt was used. All this was beyond my understanding then, but now I am blundering my way towards it. We all of us, on both planes, must recapture the teaching of form. I see this is vital and I am working hard at my lessons and enjoying them enormously. I have to come back to architecture and re-learn the meaning of the cube, the spire and the dome – all quite fascinating, and I love rubbing shoulders with the old architects of Chartres, Westminster and so on.

August 24th 1977
Yes, I'm here Cynthia. Thank you again for letting me write like this to Margaret. You can't know what a relief it is to be able just to talk in the old way on paper. Well, now I do want to tell you a little about the architecture that I've been discovering, and why form is so vital. Take the spire, it's difficult to build and the tower preceded it but both were lifting themselves up in an appeal for strength. The spire is a marvellous thing to see from this side; rays of all kind converge up at you – we can tell, or at least we can know, that the congregation are reaching out in prayer. The rays are the exact answer to prayer. Now with the dome it is quite different. Another type of ray is moulded to the curve, contacts and grows and holds the dome.

I am not yet very clear about the difference. I think the spire attracts the rapid demands, and the dome answers the call of slow concentrated meditation. Then we come down to the cube, (how you all hate the cubist building!) but the cube has its use. It's the bread and butter ray of simplicity, and can draw only one or two or even three rays at a time instead of the multiplicity which the spire and the dome are able to capture.

I went to many of our churches with our leader. It was such fun. Westminster Abbey and St. Paul's are good examples of both. I believe the English did not like the dome when it was first suggested, smacking too much of the Mosque but now I can see why we are not easily taught meditation. It's an Eastern cult. The flashy intense desire-prayers are not in our line and they can be just as strong. It all depends on the feeling you put into them – the overpowering desire for healing, or success on any plane. I might almost call it emotion, because prayer seems to emanate from what we call the emotion body. This is not an uncontrolled emotion, far from it, but a very carefully thought out complex desire given in burning ardour, that is with intense confidence to match the need. You can't pray hard and fear no result at the same time, which is what most people do. Your prayers sent out from under a spire or a dome have an added value.

I loved wandering through the old churches, and I was allowed to look back into their history and see the humble beginnings of a Power Centre. No matter how small, the Power Centre Prayer could make it grow. This shows why the old churches have so much more atmosphere of prayer and radiation; even repetition does not altogether deny entrance to the ray powers, but when the mind and heart are engaged the force is 50% higher. I am going to the East to sense the Mosques, but I am in no hurry – there are so many old and lovely vibrations in our old churches.

I have been to Edinburgh and stayed under the spell of St. Margaret's Chapel, unable to leave; the magnetism is so great. I have not yet been to Iona again, as I feel I want to learn more and have a greater command of my emotion body before I go there.

My love,
Edie

October 29th 1977
I have been working and learning all kinds of things and preparing for the great challenge, such as you have been explaining, with the advent of the Christ intermittently into your atmosphere. I have

always been tremendously interested in the physical body, and now we have another which is different, but in some ways has developed parts of the old body. We have sight and hearing on a far more extended scale and we can sense things that cannot be known in the body. For instance, when we try to visualise the procreation of life we are using the extension of the embryonic organs of the physical body. This is a power which does not belong to the Nature Spirits, so we can throw our abilities in extended form into another being, and beget thought bodies of a very advanced type. I was so excited to discover this for I had no idea at the time that it was an altogether Christlike gift to men and women.

Yes, I have seen the paper on your left, Cynthia. It is very difficult for you to understand, but it all ties in with the teaching I have received. Did I tell you that I have actually seen the Christ? You will never for one moment overlook His presence. He is secure among all of you in your vision and you will know when He appears.

We have been taught to sit in circles like you in meditation and then, when sufficient power has been generated He will appear. This is a great and exciting moment – even to speak of it like this. The first time He appeared only as a light. Then, as we gained in power and understanding, He became gradually visible and I could feel the complete presence of Christ.

30th October1977

I have been trying to assemble my thoughts so as to make them acceptable in words to you and Margaret. We use words so little that I am getting rusty at describing the things I see, and many of them have no words that I can use to give the faintest idea of the beauty and ecstasy that is literally pouring into the upper planes from still higher ones.

When I see and hear and meet people coming over who are fearful of death I just laugh at them and say, 'How can you be? This is the ultimate freedom lavishly bestowed with the power to work miracles.' I often go to meet these fearful souls and try to let in the light. It's not easy; one has to look into their auras and see the circumstances of their past lives and seek out their peculiar fears. Those who have been drowned always dread the sea, those who have been burnt, the fire, and so on but there are so many varieties.

I love meeting children because they have generally come over owing to their having no further need of the physical body and are

84

unconsciously developed souls. I have a child with me now in this room, she has been very unhappy and unloved and so I bring her into a love atmosphere of gaiety and happiness, and watch for the return of colour to her aura.

October 31st 1977
Cynthia, I see you are beset by things today, but I should like to say thank you for letting me use your powers. I want to explain to Margaret that I am in a sense just as interested as ever in all that affects her, and our long, long attachment through many lives makes an extraordinary link. We can never be separated on vital issues and I find that all the little happenings are there in my memory and brought up-to-date, but they have another scale of importance now against the background of an Eternity so vast that one's whole rhythm of life and thought moves at a different meter. I am so longing to share more, but it's groundwork of my thought-sensing which has changed, and you will all find this on coming over. I try to keep the tempo as level as I can with your thinking, but you lose so much of the real sense of life as we now know it. I do not count my days or nights and do not worry about meals, although I still have delicious fruit at times, but all physical sensations have given place to an entirely different range of feelings. For instance, you are sad when someone dies, but we are delighted and welcome them over here. I do spend a lot of time, so called, reviewing my life and the lives of others and building up a valuation of what was worthwhile on earth and what was not. I was able to put love into my cooking because I loved it, so as you say my book carries the vibration of enjoying the work. This is one of the essentials; you should enjoy your work, even love it; other senses have very little value. Now after all this sermonising I think I must say goodbye for a space. We are ever beside you. One of our sensitive bodies can respond to your lightest thought if you believe it can, but if you don't it will have no effect. And now, all love and health and blessing of congenial friends be with you from this day until we meet again in each other's vision.

Edie

November 30th 1977
Cynthia, this is exciting. Yes, here I am, longing to write again and tell Margaret more about life on this planet, but on another plane;

85

by the way, I came into your little church this morning by way of getting closer to you before writing, and I found a funeral going on of an old man who was so much interested in the whole misconception of death. 'There they are,' he said, 'all saying "poor old Albert" and never seeing me as large as life and twice as healthy! My goodness, you've no idea, at least they haven't of the blessedness of dying. I was glad when they said "he's gone".' Well, that was fun for me and I think fun for him because he wasn't seeing my side of the planet, but as I was preparing myself to talk to you and Margaret he could see me and I told him I'd been over for some time and was quite used to this lovely life and we had quite a talk and I saw his confidence returning. In fact he was excited by the prospects of life here and kept on saying, 'Why doesn't the parson tell us something of all this wonderful life ahead?' Well then I had to leave him and come home to get Margaret on her way to see you, and get in closer alignment with you both. You see I am learning my technique. I wonder what you and she feel about the coming of the new Christ age. You call it the space age but it's more than that. I'm not really a space woman yet, though I've been up quite a long way, but I do want to learn so much more about earth; I feel I can do more here, but at the same time I'm longing to see the other side of the moon. You know, the first big space flights are terrifying even for us, and one still feels very material. To go up into the rarified vibrations and lose sight of the rest of the party can be very frightening. We still have a lot of the old earthly emotions, like fear of being lost, or ceasing to be at all oneself and becoming someone else. That is the feeling with all this merging of the planes. So I hang on to 'Edie' and hold my individuality as tightly as I can, plus all I can acquire. It sounds as though I was becoming a terrible grabber, but one does need to have one's wits about one in Heaven! How I laughed when I was told just that sentence, and I pulled myself together when I realised the truth of it. Now I want to tell you how swiftly everything is changing here as well as with you. How the interchange of vibrations has made, and is making, our lives easier for us to reach you, and also I can go on to the next step of the ladder. I had never conversed with these Higher Beings such as you wrote about in the Abbey, but since then I have been on the lookout for them and this fact of expectancy has brought them within my vision. So beautiful, so immense one almost crawls under the folds of their colour rays and lies in an agony of admiration. They are so far above me that I have no words to express what they are like or how I can make a closer contact. But I have learned about the condition of mind which holds an expectant mood, patiently waiting upon God – I think this is what the Bible calls it. If you don't expect you never receive, and this works well in you just as easily as with us. If you can expect to see and learn and meet Christ or the Christed ones at Christmas, as you very well can and should, then you will. Put that in your pipe and smoke it! I am so happy, Margaret dear, that you are feeling better. Expect – no, demand – good health and you'll receive it. I am also glad that you have friends congenial to us both, and you can spread your wings and take in some of this vastness, which is most refreshing when you live on earth away from the bickering littleness of life. I am so grateful to you for all your love and care, and now for the constant thoughts that come chasing after me from you, and that my poor efforts to describe our life has awakened such interest. I am so often with our old girls with all their sex worries upon them; children, houses, money, or the lack of it. Poor darlings, what they all go through in youth. How glad I am to have done with it, and to have finished with material life for ever. Some I know yearn to go back, but I want to go on. We are all searching here, as you are, for the key to this or that question and when we find it it is usually buried with ourselves, though all the time waiting to be used. So I have spent a lot of time getting to know Edie, and bits from other lives flood up to the surface as I need them. They are all there; my Egyptian training in the temple, my Greek training with use of art and line, my Roman training in how to live. Don't forget that. We do here on this little island learn the secret of living. That is why you are going through all this industrial strife. They have to learn to live with each other in the land that protects and feeds them. It's just one of the training schools. I use my Egyptian knowledge for healing and colour power, and I think I was in Atlantis before that; but the Edie who came out of that was a very primitive being. I knew only self, and wanted nothing for others. Over the long years one has grown into other people's lives and thoughts until now, when the intimate blending of the planes makes life an entirely different creation. There is so much to realise; I'm doing this all the time. Just stay still and realise that you have inside your real self all knowledge and even some wisdom. Regulate your sight, hearing, breathing and senses; accordingly begin to draw out from within you an entirely new set of faculties. I can sense and see many thoughts that were cut off during earth life, and I stay still in the presence of the Great Power and am aware of the response within to these almighty and abiding truths. I think I've tried to write enough for today. I'll try tomorrow to elucidate what I've written.

Edie

December 1st 1977
Cynthia, I want to tell you of one of my little adventures. Yesterday I was trying to explain the groundwork of our thought and acceptance and so on. Today I want to tell you about an attempt I made into the nearer skirts of space. As you know, It's very hard work getting outside the earth's orbit and in order to do that we have to take on the second body which I have more or less managed to do. This gives me power to rise. They told me I wasn't properly dead until I had thrown off the astral body, which becomes very close to oneself and is used immediately after death. Well, with my new equipment I found I could rise much more easily off the ground and into the adjacent space, and instead of battling with the gravitational pull of earth I was taken into the aura of one of the astral planets. Just as you on earth have numerous telestars revolving in space, so we on this side have a number of floating power centres which almost resemble planets. They are of varying sizes; the one I was taken to was a mass of colour ranges, but one could seem to land on something fairly solid and breathe this wonderful other-worldly air which does not belong to earth. It was my first step outside and I asked to meet some of the inhabitants. They were mostly engaged in dealing with very severe brain damaged cases from earth who are brought in, in an unconscious state, and treated entirely by rays of colour and music. They took me onto the most beautiful plateau overlooking a lake, where the cases were all being given treatment. Having suffered unconsciousness for so long their immediate memory of the accident had been expunged, and they were thinking of it all as a lovely holiday, most of them staying quiet for some period, and then collecting themselves before being taken back to earth for the return of memory and teaching which they have either missed or gained on earth. I was thrilled to see a whole tiny planet given over to this, and I wondered whether in some future age a link, semi-physical, could not be made between our earth physical brain specialists and these

very advanced scientists. Well, there I must leave you. I was not sufficiently developed to penetrate further. It was just an expedition into space to show me one of the many semi-etheric planets which are within our grasp and are used for all kinds of purposes.

January 13th 1978
We are all chosen for certain jobs and it is our own fault if we don't look further and find ways of entering new worlds within worlds of action, thought and experience. I was first sent to one in the Highlands of Scotland, which I loved. It was in beautiful country and had been created in the first place by an old Irish saint. I thought it must be very old and said so in my mind, and was immediately answered by a tide of voluble Scottish language of my own time. I listened and realised with a physical body, and continued on the old theme of creating a power centre. I was thrilled because he was of my own time on earth, but had started in very early Christian times full of fervour and delighted to die and return with a new body to thrust the Power Centre further and further on its way. It's now a wonderful glowing Centre, but has not yet been named or recognised as such except by a few. I asked if he had any links with Iona and he laughed and said, 'Of course I was one of them at one time. We are all on the same adventure – making the earth's crust sing and glow so that there will be no night on this planet in time to come.' Think of it, no night. 'Why,' I asked, 'are we going to change our orbit round the sun?' 'Not at all, the sun will change and we shall become our own sun. All things change and we are only useful in helping these changes to function.' He was a strange aloof fellow, but I saw that my job was to pour life and yet more life into this one place and then I realised that I was pouring golden light on this centre. It circled round us in spirals and came to rest, drawing me in tighter and tighter circles until I gasped for breath. They told me to stop and lift myself out of the circle and be still – so I did and I found myself completely empty of all energy. It had been given and I must rest and re-charge the batteries before I could be of any use again. So you see we still have undiscovered tasks; they are many and varied, and monotony does not exist.

Edie

January 14th 1978

Yes, of course I should like to say more about Power Centres. Yes, there are legions of them; every tree is a Power Centre, you should bow your head in acknowledgement of the divine power in all trees: but it might be rather an effort when walking through a wood! Trees are a joy to me and now in winter, when they have no leaves, their great auras shine out over the land, fertilising the fields and giving physical and mental strength to all. I am often with the trees and I've learned to communicate with them. I can't exactly call it conversation but on a 'yes' and 'no' basis we get on very well. Each tree is a city, a community of different layers of life and vibrations. I can see and often hear the music they produce and of course the colour rays that encompass their flights of angelic-like creatures are often seen. I think they are the Devas or Nature Spirits but I'm not good at classifying them. They have a ray language which is at present quite beyond me but I shall learn it in due course. That's the lovely thing about our new brains; directly you sense an entirely new ability for which you long, that same ability becomes available to you. I don't understand if a germ of it is built into one's new body, or whether I have now acquired a sort of telephone exchange with the greater mind across my greater self, which opens the unseen doors to this new way of thinking. I am constantly amazed by the multiplicity of power lines and the extraordinary way in which the physical body seems to be insulated from them all, or nearly all.

March 1st 1978

Yes, I have been here and listened to some of your conversation. I always feel as though I were eavesdropping, but it's fun when I hear of plans to get in touch with me. Of course, I've been telling you all this during sleep. I know you can't quite take that in, but we've discussed it all and the printing of my letters. I am delighted because I feel I am in touch through them with my old pupils. They are so responsible and loving; I talk to them in their sleep-bodies too, but you'd better not tell them! They'd feel I was getting under the net of their own defences, and if I can do this in sleep why not others far less convincing? Of course they are right, so don't let's risk that issue. I can see and hear what they are saying and doing and the link is love, just straight ordinary love. The rest, those other entities, who are to be feared, have not the love vibration, quite the reverse,

90

but unfortunately the hate or mutal hate vibration draws these really evil people together from the other side and works on their minds during sleep; hence the old habit of saying one's prayers and asking for protection during sleep. I can't remember the words but various saints were commanded to watch over me during sleep, and not a bad idea either.

Well Margaret, you've recovered your health. You know I said you would, but it was very strong of you to forebear going to the surgeon. You had never been given a vision of health, so all congratulations. Now you will be with those who follow on and find that they could in this way become great initiates.

Now you want to know about starting a circle. Splendid idea, how I wish I were in the body to be able to take part. I am so full of energy that I know I could get through, and I shall do so, once you have started.

You form a spiral channel which is quite clear and you drop the names into the thinking mind of great subconscious. It's likely that you will register a potential quite out of reason with ordinary measurements. Do get this going as soon as you can.

Well! I have been in training; very extensive training for space travel. What do you think of that? I felt it couldn't be my large heavy self – often heavy in mind as well as body – when I was going to be trained for this; but once undertaken I couldn't stop. It's the most exciting thing I've ever done. First they asked me to use the earth currents generated on the surface, which we all use (and you could too) which don't extend very high. Then I was shoved, yes shoved, into another layer of currents – wireless waves which they call the heavy-side layer – then I felt quite different and not very comfortable or amenable. I couldn't direct them and I felt I might be going off anywhere. I was scared, I really was. I asked for help which came immediately telling me not to feel alone in space which is enormously full of all kinds of light. I hadn't noticed any – but that was my fault. One can switch on one's senses and one's feeling of adjacent things, but when I am focused on one thing I can't do it at all. Some have to switch off everything and just listen, which I did; and then I saw and heard one of my guides saying 'Don't be afraid, we'll never leave you.' So I just waited and stopped. I was swinging about in space – quite pleasant but rather rootless – wondering what would happen next. They told me to trust them and they would steer me on to one of the nearer etheric planets. This happened quite

91

quickly and I felt a wonderful release from tension, which they said was the pull of the earth, always unwilling to leave her children; but once the tension was released they said I would not feel it again. So there I was on an etheric planet. It was delightful – a sort of fairyland of colour to me, while beautiful nymph-like creatures swarmed everywhere and torrents of music came to me on beams of colour. Very confusing at first. I wanted to receive one or other, but not both together. I longed for quiet and I was given just that. A lovely peaceful brook in some way absorbed both the unfocused music and the colour, and I could just stay on the ground and watch the beams (which had dazzled me) condense into rainbows over the water; all the sound was absorbed into the bubble and swish of the brook. That is what all brooks do everywhere a voice told me, but here it is more intense. They said, 'Now you must sleep and recover from your experience and later we will help you back on to your own plane.' I felt a great longing to get back and without a moment's pause there I was on the plane of my development, quite near the earth with all bodies in tune and exultant over the release, yet feeling that one big step had been taken towards space movement.

I can't write any more today but I wanted you to know that I have made the grade and am on my way to become space-conscious.

All love,

Edie

April 14th 1978
Cynthia, I am so happy to meet you here again. It is magical to find that two lives can really become one. I have been learning about this, and it is taking me a long time. I have, like all of you, lived many different lives, and now I reassemble the experience again through each life and to adjust my present way of thinking in order to accept more primitive scales and accept the fundamental teaching gained each time. Some were very rough lives and I rather hated going through the feeling of life as a hunter or a fisherman, and of course very often as a soldier or a sailor. I have often been a man; my feminine lives were considerably fewer and not at all happy.

I loved the width and space of a man's life, in spite of all the hard work and the many adventures and assassinations. Oh dear, how often I have planned these and been assassinated myself. Our lives were very violent. I can feel my French womanly self more easily but

I was cold and remorseless even then. It was really only in my last life that I attained the understanding of the human being. Margaret you gave me so much of the real feminine touch and the way to overcome patiently. In former days we overcame stormfully and this tore us to pieces. I was in Greece and Rome and Egypt, then I was in North America among the Red Indians, and it is their wisdom which I am now weaving into my finer body. I have to become that which I then was and relate that wisdom only to the highest motives. Over and over again I failed but the Christ puts us on our feet, and we reluctantly try once more.

Seeing Margaret revived in me a lot of memories. We were tied up with ancient worships and this is a theme which I *must* learn about. I must also *see* the pure love worship which was so rare in those former days. All, or nearly all, ancient and modern worship aims at *getting* but seldom *giving*. This was something we learnt together in Egypt, and they all laughed at us, but we persisted and gained tremendous mental power over others and thus became 'hooked' on power. This was my downfall over and over again. Power! You've no idea how insidious power becomes.

So, on coming over here we have *no* power, except in ourselves and in those we serve. Its all very difficult to understand, and more so to describe. But life remains one enormous glorious adventure, and free. I am not going to write more tonight except to tell Margaret that her sense of coming into a blind alley will pass, and she will recover and be eager for the fight. This is the point which I have now reached, and she will turn the corner and reach a state of growing happiness. I shall be there too, now and all the time.

Edie

April 15th 1978
Thank you, Cynthia, that was a lovely introduction, and full of vital power. How I loved seeing the rays pouring into you both.

I have a great feeling for the earth and the sky, and like your brother I do realise that I don't really belong to the earth. But do any of us? Aren't we really members of a much wider horizon, going out and out into the depths of Space? I am aware now, having made my first debut into Space, that we are only at the beginning of our evolution.

I have met and talked to a number of wonderful people, like Father Andrew, who as you know, is a Christed one, and he tells me that there is no limit – but *no* limit – to the functions, distances and immensities of this universe which, as seen by an astronomer, is more or less boundless – but that is only as seen from the physical plane. Then think of the enormous quantity of finer planes interpenetrating the physical and extending to goodness knows where. Our own sense of divinity becomes enlarged beyond all conception.

I can speak of these things to you, Cynthia, and to Margaret, but for many, even over here, the sense of boundlessness is very frightening. But why should we ask to limit God's power? It doesn't seem to me to be either necessary or reasonable. I want to go on and on, yet at the same time continue to possess this amazing thread of contact with all whom I love and have loved, and shall learn to love in the future, thus making a solid group united through love power.

How important it is to learn to give ourselves absolutely!

PRAYER

Now this prayer is the gist of the whole of our contact. You have a faculty for throwing your thoughts out andd aligning them with mine. You call t prayer for lack of a better word. But I want to explain that this contact is made in so many ways.

It consists of the opening of the aura to the universal spirit of God; and then the directing of it by the use of that same spirit to the individual you want to contact.

People who love one another very deeply are in a constant state of prayer because love on this scale is God Power.

I can't stress the importance of this factor too much and the knowledge of my active life here, and with you, has helped very considerably to keep the force a strong and living current between us.

We all live, as it were, like fish in an aquarium, swimming about in the water of God's Power – without it we should lie on the bottom and die.

With it, and with it alone, we work. When you want to help someone you send thoughts God-wards, and to someone on this side if they exist, who knows the individual, to make the instant contact, and this I can do IF I am given the power and the directive.

I know this is the darkest hour, but it always comes before the dawn, and you may feel quite, quite certain that the dawn will be soul shattering in wonder and DELIGHT.